T0381525

OBSERVATIONS

2000-2009

by Martin Green

iUniverse, Inc.
New York   Bloomington

OBSERVATIONS
2000-2009

Copyright © 2010 by Martin Green

iUniverse books may be ordered through booksellers or by contacting:
iUniverse
1663 Liberty Drive
Bloomington, IN 47403
www.iuniverse.com
1-800-Authors (1-800-288-4677)

ISBN: 978-1-4502-3007-0 (pbk)
ISBN: 978-1-4502-3008-7 (ebk)

Printed in the United States of America
iUniverse rev. date: 5/25/10

FOREWORD

At the end of 1997, my wife Beverly and I moved into Del Webb's first Northern California retirement community, Sun City Roseville, just outside of Sacramento. Our move was on December 29th, one day before my birthday. At that time, I'd been retired from the State of California, where I'd been primarily a research analyst, for seven years. I'd also become a free-lance writer, first for an "alternative" weekly newspaper called Suttertown News, non-paying, so it was a volunteer job; then also for the Neighbors section of the Sacramento Bee, which I was happy to find did pay its free-lancers, so I had a paying job.

About two years later, in early 2000, someone from a newspaper called the Sun Senior News, which was mailed to Sun City residents at the start of each month, came to interview me. This was because I'd established and was the first president of the New Yorkers club in Sun City. During the course of the interview, it came out that I wrote for Sacramento Bee Neighbors (the Suttertown News by then had expired). The interviewer then suggested that I might also write for the Sun Senior News.

I sat down at my computer and in 15 or 20 minutes wrote what I called "Observations After Living Two Years in Sun City" and mailed it in to the Sun Senior News. It was printed in the March issue and was the start of my "Observations" writing for the Sun Senior News. "Observations" wasn't a monthly column at first and I could only find two more columns for the balance of 2000. I'm not sure exactly when but eventually "Observations" did become a regular monthly feature. (I later started another monthly feature called "Favorite Restaurants," which, like "Observations." is ongoing at this date)

This book presents a collection of "Observations" through the end of 2009. To the best of my ability, I've put them in chronological order. I wanted to do this book primarily to preserve, at least for some period of time, my work. I was also interested in how my "Observations" had evolved, if they had, over a period of about ten years. I knew that they'd gone from a focus on Sun City to the world in general and that they allowed me to express my opinions on a number of matters. They also allowed me, as the reader will see, to vent about things that annoyed me and about some things that seemed more than just annoying. So, all in all, I enjoyed writing them. I hope readers will enjoy reading them.

2001 OBSERVATIONS

The observation about Sun City that caused the most comment was the one that the parking lot at the Lodge (the center of Sun City activities) was always full, whether anything was going on there or not and yet when you went into the Lodge it was almost always empty. Over the years, several theories to explain this have been offered to me: people going on bus trips departing from the Lodge leave their cars parked there; people go into the adjoining Fitness Center; people park and return home by some other means. None of these explanations seems convincing, so the question of where all those people go remains one of life's everlasting mysteries.

The other observation that stands out after ten years is that people at Sun City (and by extension all senior citizens) like to eat out and travel. This observation was based on the fact that eating out and travel were the subjects of most conversations among Sun City residents. My column on "Favorite Restaurants," which started later, was based on this observation. And, as will be seen, travel became a favorite topic for future "Observations."

Two Years at Sun City Roseville

Here are some observations after having been at Sun City Roseville for two years.

The city of San Jose doesn't have any senior citizens left because they've all moved up here.

The entire Bay Area doesn't have any senior citizens left except for Willie Brown because they've all moved up here.

After Willie Brown retires from being mayor of San Francisco, he'll move up here.

After Bill Clinton retires from being president of the United States, he'll move . . . no, sorry Bill, you'll still be too young.

Everyone at Sun City Roseville has a dog and walks it at the crack of dawn.

The parking lot at the Lodge is always filled up with cars because there's always some activity going on there.

The parking lot at the Lodge is always filled up with cars even when nothing is going on there.

The parking lot at the Lodge is always filled up with cars but when you go into the Lodge it's almost empty. Where did all the people go? If anyone knows, e-mail me.

Everyone here e-mails everyone else, starting with when they get home from walking the dog.

Whenever two people at Sun City meet and they have some common interest they form a club.

At last count, there were 58 chartered clubs at Sun City.

There's a club for women named Barbara. Really.

Thousands of people here play golf.

Del Webb discovered something when he figured out that retired people are crazy for golf. If you build a golf course with a retirement community around it, they will come.

The golfers say they golf because it gets them outdoors in the fresh air and sunshine and because of the good fellowship. I personally think it's because they get to zip around Sun City in those nifty little golf carts.

Everyone at Sun City likes to eat. Almost all club events involve eating. Sometimes it's a potluck. Sometimes food is catered in from outside. Sometimes it's a breakfast, or a lunch or a dinner at the Lodge restaurant or some outside eating place.

One of the local TV stations just had a news segment on the booming restaurant business in and around Roseville. It's no coincidence.

Quite a few Sun City residents either go to the Fitness Center here or say they're going or thinking about going. This may be related to everyone liking to eat.

Everyone at Sun City travels. And they travel everywhere. The other week my wife and I were at a lunch, where else. All the other couples at our table had either just returned from somewhere or were about to leave for somewhere.

One couple had been to China. One was going to Tahiti. One had been to Australia and New Zealand. One had bicycled through Europe. Bicycled? I think I've seen them at the Fitness Center. One had hiked through the Alps. Definitely regulars at the Fitness Center.

The Sun City Travel Club is planning the first ever senior citizens climb of Mount Everest. No, just kidding. I think I'm kidding anyway.

As everyone at Sun City likes to eat and to travel, everyone likes to go on cruises.

There must something fascinating about cruising through the Panama Canal because everyone has done it or wants to do it. Do they give out a prize? A free set of dishes (they used to do that at the movies)?

One of our neighboring couples has been on 14 cruises. Their last one was really adventurous, up, or down, the Amazon. Come to think of it, I haven't seen them for a while. No, it must just be a long cruise. Maybe they're also going through the Panama Canal.

Sun City Roseville residents don't only eat, travel, cruise and form clubs. They are many admirable people here who volunteer to help others. They drive, visit, take food to sick neighbors, provide support, raise funds and donate.

But where do all those people parked at the Lodge go?

Still More Sun City Observations

Back by popular demand—at least two readers that I know of--here are still more Sun City observations. While my wife and I were waiting for our Sun City house to be built we rented in the Crosswood area in Citrus Heights and almost every evening walked the two miles around Crosswood Circle, possibly the nicest walk in the Sacramento area, with large trees, a stream which was home to many ducks and a grassy area populated by tame rabbits. When we moved here about 2 ½ years ago, we were worried about finding pleasant walks in Sun City, with construction still going on and trees and front yards just being planted.

I was reminded of this when I read Cleo Kocol's excellent feature on "Wild Sun City" in May's Sun Senior News. We needn't have worried because, living on Timberrose, we are within easy walking distance of the pond by the golf course and Schoolhouse Park. We like to make a daily trip to the pond to check on the heron and the egret which are usually there. Over the winter, there were about a dozen geese and lately there've been ducks. We've also been walking the other way to Del Webb to see the family of ducks on the golf course pond there. The golfers and nearby residents must be spoiling this duck family because as soon as they see us coming they waddle up to the sidewalk, expecting to be fed. Sun City of course abounds in many other forms of bird life. Doves especially seem to feel at home here as they can be either seen or heard at all times. As for Schoolhouse Park, it makes for a destination when walking but I've never seen anyone much there, not even Cleo, and I wonder if something can be done to put the park to better use.

Aside from the wildlife, Sun City's front yards are, like the ducks, no longer in their infancy but approaching adolescence. Shrubs, flowers and ground cover abound and the trees are beginning to look like trees instead of sticks. We're noticing more and more For Sale signs. At one time, everyone was moving into Sun City. Now some are moving out.

In connection with this, I've heard several people remark recently that some of the committees and clubs are looking for new nominees for office as the original pioneers who got things going ease off on their activities. Maybe it's time for a second generation of "doers" to come to the fore.

This brings me to observing once again that Sun City has an amazing number of talented people. Cleo Kocol, novelist, performer and president of the Scribes, is one, as are the members of the Scribes Drama Club. Readers who've attended the recent art show know we have many gifted artists; those who went to the recent Singers concert know we have an outstanding chorus and members of those clubs for whom they've performed know we have remarkable dancers of all kinds.

Finally, I've recently had first-hand experience of what I'd been told was a common Sun City addiction. This is the love affair certain Sun Cityites have with their computers, so intense that they can't bear to be separated from them and so are on them all day. Meanwhile, everything else gets neglected and people trying to call them find they always get a strange noise on the phone line and can't get through. In the case of our household, my wife was presented with a supposedly "obsolete" laptop computer that our future daughter-in-law obtained from her workplace. Within 24 hours, she was throwing out terms like "search engine," "e-mail address" and "where did that cursor go?" Well, there's no denying the impact of the new technology. My wife is already exchanging e-mails with our future daughter-in-law's family, who reside in Limerick, Ireland (yes, the Limerick of "Angela's Ashes") and I suppose that's a good thing. I suppose it's also a good thing that all those salespersons who used to call us during dinnertime are now getting funny noises in their ears. If anyone wants to get in touch with me, please send a message by carrier pigeon or one of those doves.

I see that, as noted above, it didn't take long for me to write an "Observations about travel, this one about a cruise my wife Beverly and I took on a Mississippi steamboat with the Sun City travel club. After I retired and before we moved to Sun City, Beverly and I had gone on a number of bus tours in Europe and the States. Cruises appeal to seniors because they're not as strenuous as bus tours and because you don't have to continually unpack and then pack again. You put your things in your cabin and then relax for the rest of the trip.

Cruisin' on the Mississippi

In my piece on observations after two years at Sun City Roseville (March's Sun Senior News) I noted that as everyone here likes to eat and to travel, everyone likes to go on cruises. My wife and I not being exceptions to this rule, we went on a Mississippi riverboat cruise with the Sun City travel club in early March. I didn't actually keep a diary of the cruise but if I had these might have been some excerpts from it.

Day 1. we had the first of our big cruise ship dinners, with everyone having bread pudding in whiskey sauce for dessert. My wife and I had bread pudding twice in New Orleans before sailing but you can't have enough of it. If the Timbers restaurant would make their bread pudding with whiskey sauce it would taste much better. We compared our cabins and all agreed it would help to be a contortionist in using the bathrooms. All the ladies are wearing the colorful beads they throw out on the pre-Mardi Gras parades so they've either been agile enough to catch them or have bought them in stores.

Day 2. almost everyone on the boat is on the elderly side. As at Sun City, the cruise line tries to provide daylong activities, walking around the deck, bingo after lunch, other games in the afternoon. After dinner, to a show and then dancing to the Dick Jurgens band, which I kind of remember from long ago. The band played songs from the 40's and 50's, when, as somebody said, you could understand the words and they weren't obscene. What price progress.

Day 4. A shore excursion to visit an ante-bellum mansion. Our guide said that just as rich people today buy expensive cars, rich Southerners used to build mansions. Yet another big cruise dinner. Our waiter, Felix, always says, I hope you have room for dessert. If not, make room. Nobody is ordering bread pudding any more. After dinner, Felix always treats us to a song. We of course think we have the best waiter there. I don't know if any of the other waiters sing but I'm sure all the other tables also think their waiter is something special.

Day 5. the Dick Jurgens band has been replaced by Sammy Kaye's. Everyone has heard of Swing and Sway with Sammy Kaye. A few of the band members look old enough to have played with Sammy Kaye and, sure enough, they had. We've taken to watch the dancing every night. Almost all the dancers have white, gray or no hair and many are, shall we say, a little overweight, but they all step sprightly along. One strange lady usually dances by herself, always with a little smile on her face. Two of our group, both named Lou, are on the dance floor every night. One Lou, I'm told, is 92 and the other, I'm told, is a mere 82 and was the most decorated man in his battalion during World War II. If I thought it would make me as trim and energetic as the two Lous I'd take up dancing myself.

Day 6. This is Fat Tuesday, Mardi Gras day in New Orleans and also on our boat. One of our group, Audie, is selected to be Mardi Gras queen and she worries about the crown slipping off her head. But at the big Mardi Gras procession, after the dancing that night, she looks fine in her cape and crown and does Sun City proud. All of the ladies in our group, and a lot of the men, wear their colorful beads.

Day 7. At the buffet lunch today, the Captain sat down with us. He's tall and handsome and most nights comes to the dances. I speculated that he might be a "fake" captain and that some short, fat, unshaven guy is actually driving the boat. But the Captain is smart as well as handsome and knows his stuff so I was wrong again.

Day 8. Last day of the cruise. The Mardi Gras beads have all disappeared. Where do they go for the rest of the year? We're all ready to get back to Sun City. Enough Southern mansions, enough tiny bathrooms, enough eating huge meals. We have to get to the Fitness Center.

Day 11, post-cruise. We've been back three days. No more being waited on hand-and-foot. No more entertainment and dancing. It's raining. Gas prices are going sky-high. It's time to go on another cruise.

A more serious observation: it's curiously affecting to watch the elderly couples on the dance floor. Maybe that strange lady who dances by herself is smiling as she thinks of the young men who used to escort her. Maybe those gray-haired couples are thinking of the old days, possibly during World War II, when the man was going overseas and they wondered what was in store for them and maybe when they return to their cabins they've rekindled the feelings of long ago.

In my Sun City observations piece, I noted that while the Lodge parking lot was always filled with cars, often the Lodge itself was empty and wondered where all the people went. One reader suggests that all our garages are so stuffed with golf clubs and carts, work tables and tools, plus things collected for charity drives that we leave our cars in the parking lot and go home. Any other theories?

The observation below that stands out for me is that seniors come early, usually very early, to all events. This was true back then and continues to be true. As recently as last month, Beverly and I arrived at 8:50 for a bus trip scheduled to leave at nine. Needless to say, we were the last ones on the bus and sat in the last row. The same thing invariably happens when we attend a club lunch, go to lunch or dinner with a group or go to any other Sun City function. When we arrive on time, or even a little ahead of time, we're always late.

I also noted those times of forgetfulness which are called "senior moments" and which we who live here refer to as "Sun City moments." I had those moments back then and have them now, only more often.

More Observations About Sun City

The response to my column on Observations About Sun City After Two Years was so great--my wife liked it--that here are some further observations. In that first Observations piece, I noted that Sun City residents are invariably up at dawn. "I like to have a cup of coffee and read the newspaper" is the usual explanation. My wife is a notable exception, being a night owl and a late riser, who . . . Uh, oh, better leave it at that. The point is that the minority who are late risers should do what every other group at Sun City with a shared interest has done, form a club, meet for late brunches, have parties centered around watching the 11 o'clock news, and maybe even watch Nightline at 11:30 so they can report to the rest of us on Ted Koppel's hair.

In keeping with this early-hour lifestyle, Sun City residents invariably come to all events early. If there's an event at the Lodge scheduled for seven PM, then the line to get in will start forming at six. By 6:45, all places are taken and any latecomers will have to stand. Why this compulsion to be early? Maybe it's because our generation was brought up by parents who constantly admonished us not to be tardy. Yes, we used to be sent to the principal's office for being tardy, nor for carrying a gun to school. Or maybe it's because, since we're old enough to know all the catastrophes life can bring, we feel we must leave early, just in case. Or maybe it's just because we know everyone else will get there early so we'd better do so ourselves.

Del Webb planned for Sun City to be an active community and they've more than succeeded. All of the residents here, especially the women, are busy at all times. When two or more women want to get together there's a great flurry of getting out the appointment books or those little calendars they carry around and a lengthy discussion of what few dates are still available. Then the meeting is set for some day two or three months in the future and they all say, I hope nothing else comes up before then. As for us men, we usually say, I'll have to check with my wife about that.

To continue on this theme, it's not uncommon for Sun City residents to say, Boy, I'm busier now than before I retired. And I thought we'd reached the time of life when, free of the cares of work and raising a family, we could relax and contemplate things. Maybe a Contemplation Club should be formed. Of course, it seems we're never free from family cares. We still worry, not only about our parents who are of nursery home age, but about those now middle-aged (the kids) of ours.

I can't end these observations without mentioning "Sun City moments," which refer to moments of temporary forgetfulness. You rarely go by a day here without hearing somebody say, "I'm having a Sun City moment." I suppose that's why all the women carry appointment books or little calendars. I'd say something more about this but I hear my wife calling that we have to go a one o'clock meeting (how could I have forgotten that?) and it's already noon.

Just one last thing: in last month's Cruisin' on the Mississippi piece, I referred to the two dancing Lou's. I'm told one is a Lew, his last name is Skaug and he's only 91, not 92. The other Lou is Lou Overcramer. Lew Skaug told me all this, plus that he'll be dancing on the Mississippi Queen again next year.

2001 OBSERVATIONS

I have a number of "Observations" looking back at the previous year or looking ahead at the year to come. The "Observations" below is the first I wrote on looking back. The year 2000, or 2YK as it was known, was the one where the world was supposed to come to an end because our computers couldn't cope with the change from the 1900's to the 2000's. It was also the year of the "hanging chad" election between Gore and Bush, so possibly it seemed like the end of the world to Democrats.

Observations Looks Back at 2000

January: On New Year's Eve 1999, the talk was all about Y2K. Remember. Would our water stop running, our electricity go out, planes fall from the sky (as depicted on one TV show), our social security checks stop coming? None of these disasters came about and by Super Bowl Sunday Y2K was all but forgotten.

February: We usually have a false spring in this area, but the weather was dismal. Maybe it was because one of the truly great men of our time, Charles Schultz, creator of Peanuts, passed away. His unique comic strip brightened our days for years. One of the few good things the media has done recently is to continue to run Peanuts as it's hard to imagine starting our day without it.

March: My wife and myself went on a Mississippi River cruise. It was not only a cruise down the Mississippi but a cruise down memory lane. Entertainment on our ship was provided by the Dick Jergens Band, the Swing and Sway with Sammy Kaye Band and none other than the Ink Spots. In the case of at least the Sammy Kaye Band, some were the original musicians, older than their audience. These performers were a reminder of the hectic days of World War II, the post-war times when we were getting our first jobs and houses and starting to raise our families. They were also a reminder of when songs had melodies and lyrics were poetic and not obscene.

April: Spring, baseball, taxes. But the big story (remember) was Elian Gonzalez. Little did we know then that Florida was to be the scene of an even bigger story later on. Maybe all the media hoopla over "little" Elian should have forewarned us. Wonder what he's doing now?

May: All of those recent Bay Area emigres found out that we can have 100-degree days even this early. But the month's low point came when our Sacramento Kings lost that fifth game in Los Angeles. Wait until next year, guys.

June: We had our first appliance breakdown. Needless to say, it was our air-conditioner and it happened right before a big heat wave. Well, that's what living in the Valley is all about.

July: We thought we'd get away from the Valley heat when we went with the Travel Club to Ashland, only to have 100-plus temperatures there. But the heat didn't spoil our pleasure in seeing Hamlet and The Man Who Came to Dinner. This last, which dated back to the 1930's, was still amazingly funny. Nowadays, the overbearing Man Who Came to Dinner, who was a famous radio host, would be a TV talk show host. Rush Limbough?

August: Gas went to $2 a gallon. Even worse, The Survivors became our summer obsession. I must admit my wife and I became hooked. I rooted for crusty Rudy. Is it any surprise in our cynical times that Richard was the winner? His obvious new career is political consultant.

September: The Survivors gave way to way to a true TV fiasco, the Olympics. We knew the winners beforehand and even if we wanted to watch a certain event they wouldn't tell us when it would be on. The only certainty was that the day's big even would be the last one shown.

October: we went back East on a fall foliage (leaf-peeping) tour and then for a visit to New York. Yes, transplanted Easterners, the leaves back there do change colors, just as we remember, and they were well worth peeping at. As for New York, there's still no place like it, maybe because it has more of everything. The buildings are taller, the traffic is worse (except maybe for Cairo), the people are louder, the pace is faster, there are more restaurants, more museums, more plays, more of everything. No, I don't want to move back there, but it's always exciting to visit.

November: Hmmm, can't remember anything happening this month.

December: Just kidding, of course. I've been waiting for a resolution to the big election crisis before completing this year 2000 review and it came just in time to meet my deadline. All of the apt things that could be said about this five-week extravaganza have been said by Leno and Letterman. So I'll just add that I think everyone is glad it's finally over. Meanwhile, we have the threat of power outages, and isn't this where we came in at the start of the year with Y2K. Like Y2K, let's hope this doesn't materialize. With that, happy holidays and on to 2001.

Below is the first "Observations" I wrote about life's little annoyances, or LLA's, although I didn't refer to them as "LLA's" at that time. In discussing annoyances associated with my HMO, which haven't changed in the interim, I mentioned their automated phone system, definitely one of life's greatest annoyances. I also noted as an annoyance the was some young people condescendingly talk to us senior citizens. This also hasn't changed and is still just as annoying.

Observations Looks At Life's Little Annoyances

Last month's Observations took a pretty optimistic look at the year 2001. It even said that the Governor, the Legislature and the utility companies would come up with a plan to supply California with power at no increase in rates. Okay, let's say it was wildly optimistic. That New Year's Eve champagne I had before writing it must have been more potent than I realized. Well, almost two months of 2001 have passed and, as we contend with rolling blackouts and anticipate with dread our next utility bills, it's time to get back to reality. Everyone has had a say about the power crisis and other big issues (such as Temptation Island and Survivors II) so this month Observations will take a look at some of the little annoyances of life, daily hassles that we all undergo, and where possible even make a few suggestions for dealing with them.

Like most seniors, I find that I'm going to see the doctor more often and, as the HMOs in our area, have more and more seniors enrolled, I'm spending more and more time in the waiting room. I don't mind this too much as I'm prepared for waiting and always bring a book of sufficient length to see me through. What's really bothersome is waiting in that chilly little cubicle, usually while only partially dressed, while people pass back and forth out in the hall beyond your closed door. After a while, you're unable to concentrate on even the most interesting book because you're wondering what's going on out there and if they've completely forgotten you. My suggestion, if they must put you in that little cubicle, is to at least provide coffee and refreshments plus possibly music to make the time go by more pleasantly. If they take this simple step, maybe patients' blood pressure wouldn't be ten or 20 points higher than usual when they finally get around to taking it.

While in the middle of writing this, I encountered another annoying thing with my HMO, the matter of being referred. In mid-November, my doctor referred me to the physical therapy department. When two months passed and nothing had happened I called physical therapy and was told they had no record of my being referred. I called the doctor, not the doctor himself, of course but a number and after navigating the automated answering system got through to a human being, who told me that in order to be referred I had to see the doctor again. I wanted to discuss my medication with him anyway so didn't protest and made another appointment. He assured me he had referred me, but would refer me again and if I hadn't heard in a few days to call physical therapy. Needless to say, I didn't hear and needless to say when I called they'd still never heard of me. So back to calling the doctor's number and the automated answering system. (After two months, I finally made it).

What to do about this seemingly insoluble problem? The answer is obvious. What this HMO (and all organizations like it) should do is hire a team of senior citizens. As we all know, seniors are conscientious, reliable and dependable. As soon as a referral is made, a member of this team takes it to the appropriate department. Then there's no question; it will be done. In fact, the automated answering system should be replaced by another team of seniors. They will handle all calls as if they came from their grandchildren and see to it that everyone gets the proper attention, nagging the HMO until this is done.

Besides going to doctors more as you get older, I find you're also taking more and more pills. Possibly the worst part about pills, other than having to remember when to take them, is trying to penetrate the packaging to get at them. I suppose this dates back to the Tylonol poison incidents and I know it's a good thing to prevent would-be poisoners from getting into medications. But possibly they've gone too far and it's time to consider some form of packaging that would be safe and that at the same time doesn't require a Swiss army knife or a screwdriver to get into. Then you'd have a good chance of taking your blood pressure pills before your blood pressure goes through the roof (while waiting in those cubicles). Of course, impossible-to-open packaging isn't confined to medications but applies to everything nowadays. I recently bought some batteries, to make sure our flashlights work in the coming blackouts, and in the time it took to open them a rolling blackout could have rolled through and gone. I'm sure those astronauts don't have to contend with such packaging way out in space, so come on, NASA scientists, let the general public in on whatever it is that's used for them.

Although I'm seeing the doctor more often and taking more pills, I still don't consider myself to be in my dotage. That's why it's annoying when some young person, whether it's the receptionist at the HMO, the checkout person at the store where you buy those pills or anyone else, addresses you in the fake syrupy tones usually reserved for a small child or a pet. It's as if they're saying, "Oh, isn't that old geezer cute. He can still get around on his own." It's even more annoying when that young person, whom you've never seen before, calls you by your first name, as if you're a life-long friend.

I don't know of any quick solution for dealing with this as these young people probably mean well and we're from a generation taught to be polite. In any case, there's a whole catalogue of daily annoyances—drivers who go too fast or too slow and don't signal turns, rude waitpersons, customers who hold up lines, Richard Hatch, TV commercials, etc.—which just have to be endured. But there is a way to reduce the stress caused by all of these annoyances. In one of Muriel Spark's novels, the heroine, a young lady who works in publishing, is conversing with a retired general who wants to write his memoirs but who says he can't concentrate. She advises him to get a cat. The serenity naturally radiated by a cat, she tells him, will enable him to concentrate. A few years later, she receives a copy of the general's book, dedicated to her. On the back cover is a picture of the general with his cat Grumpy.

I'm not sure about concentration but a cat's natural serenity will help to dispel stress. When you return home from the doctor, the store, the DMV, wherever, and your TV or radio tells you a rolling blackout is imminent, your cat will jump into your lap, purr and the annoyances will melt away. So, if you don't already have one, take Muriel Spark's advice: get a cat.

August 2001 Observations

This Observations is the first I had comparing the present with the "good old days." I looked at movies, television, music and sport and in each case came down on the side of earlier times. I know the good old days weren't always all that good, but I haven't changed my mind By the way, by this time I'd gotten away from writing strictly about Sun City matters.

I won't argue that everything in the "good old days" was that good. I vividly remember going to the dentist, who lived down the street, and having my teeth filled without benefit of Novocain. Neither did we have the benefit of fluoride. Health care in general was in the dark ages as compared to today. Nobody ever heard of kidney transplants, heart transplants, knee and hip replacements, valium, Prozac or Viagra. I'm sure our appliances weren't as good. Airplanes were propelled by propellers, not by jets. We didn't have microwaves, CDs. VCRs or color TVs, not to mention cell phones and computers.

But despite all of our modern advances, lately I've been thinking that many things from what now seem to be the prehistoric times of the 1940s and 1950s were better than they are today. One of the things that set off this thinking was that we haven't gone to the movies more than once or twice this year. Am I the only one or have movies gotten really terrible? There's the same old jumble of teen-age "comedies," featuring sex and obscenity, "thrillers" with the most advanced special effects and the dumbest possible plots, and sequels to sequels to sequels.

The old studio system certainly had its faults but it managed to turn out reasonably good movies that we could go to every week. And look at the stars we had. Bogart, Spencer Tracy, Gable, Hepburn, Bette Davis, Audrey Hepburn, Gregory Peck, Gary Cooper and on and on. One thing, I think, is for sure. The actual event of going to a movies was much more satisfying than it is nowadays. The movie houses were palaces. There were ushers. People (most of them) didn't talk. The sound didn't shatter your eardrums. The prices were reasonable. They even gave away free dishes.

I wonder if even the old television shows, in snowy black and white and on tiny screens, were in a way better than the stuff we get on our huge color sets, soon to be digital, today. I remember Show of Shows, with Sid Caeser, Imogine Coca (recently, and regrettably, deceased), Carl Reiner and Hal Morris. Surely, their sketches were works of art. Then there were "sitcoms" like the Lucille Ball Show, The Odd Couple, Mary Tyler Moore, Taxi, the first Bob Newhart Show and Mash. Recently, we saw "Marty," getting the video from the Sun City library, and I was reminded that it was first on television, as were dozens of other dramas, all put on live. And who can forget the live Playhouse 90.

Then there's music. Remember when we had songs with melodies you could hum or whistle and with lyrics that told a story. In many cases, as with Cole Porter and Ira Gershwin, the lyrics were witty. In others, in songs by Lerner and Lowe or Jerome Kern, the lyrics sometimes approached poetry. I don't have to tell you what we have today. One comment I've gotten is: "Any kid with a few guitar lessons can get up on a stage and howl and gyrate, but the result isn't music, it's noise." It's no wonder that half of the hit shows on Broadway are revivals of the old musicals of the 40's and 50's. Come to think of it, where would the Music Circus be without those shows.

One more area I want to touch on and that's sports Now there's no question that today's athletes are bigger, stronger and faster than those back in our day. But rooting for your team was a lot more satisfying because you knew who your players were. For example, in New York when I grew up the Yankees had Mantle, the Giants had Mays and the Dodgers had Snyder and you could argue from one season to the next who was the best centerfielder. As I write this, Jason Williams is already gone from the Kings and the future of Chris Webber is anybody's guess. It's been fun seeing the Kings, after countless painful years, finally develop into a good team that was also fun to watch. Now, come fall, we'll be rooting for a different team, no more J Will and possibly no more C Webb or Doug Christie. And of course the same is true no matter what the sport and no matter which team you follow.

Well, movies, television, music and sports. I think that covers enough territory for one month. I've had some interesting comments from people I exchange e-mail with on the issue of today versus the good old days. Maybe there's even a good case to be made for today.

I'm writing this on my computer and will e-mail it in. How did we get along without our computers in the pre-tech age? .

Then came 9/11 and of course my Observations had to be about that. I observed that 9/11 had brought our country's people and wondered how long this would continue. I think we all know the regrettable answer to that.

Observations After September 11ᵗʰ

Although this is written a month after the terrorist attacks of September 11, the events of that day which shook our nation are still very much in everyone's mind. At the same time, President Bush is urging people to resume flying, Leno and Letterman are back, the new television season (after a week's delay) has started, David Barry is writing funny columns again, so it's time to get on with it.

One observation on September 11 is how its reverberations have spread out to affect so many lives. Readers may remember that in my last Observations I mentioned the wedding of our youngest son Chris to Florinda (Flindie) McCarthy on September 15 in Monterey, an international event bringing together family and friends from Ireland, Australia, New York City, the South and California. The disruption in airline travel resulted in some two dozen people being unable to come, although everyone tried.

There were successes and failures. Flindie's parents had flown in from Limerick the week before. My sister and her husband flew in from New York the Sunday before. But a bridesmaid from Ireland and another from Australia (the Irish seem to go to Australia just as Americans used to go West) couldn't make it. Neither could my three nephews from New York. But my wife's brother and his wife flew out from Florida the day before the wedding and then Flindie's two brothers, along with one fiance and one girl friend, literally just made it, speeding into the parking lot as our bus was about to leave Santa Cruz for Monterey. I report all this because I suspect that many readers have already experienced similar ups and downs in their lives and I'm sure we'll all continue to experience them in days to come.

Another observation: September 11 has not only affected all of our lives, some of its consequences are likely to be odd and unexpected. It was obvious that air travel and anything affected by it was going to be dramatically impacted. But, among other things, New York's Mayor Gugliani became a national hero, several Broadway shows closed down, the TV show "West Wing": cancelled its opening episode and ex-President Clinton praised President Bush.

As has happened after every attack against us, the most notable consequence of September 11 has been a remarkable pulling-together of our country's people. This is evidenced in the outpouring of donations to victims of the terrorist attacks, the many patriotic rallies all over, and Congress's support of the President. Can this continue in a "war" that we've been warned is going to be protracted with possibly no visible victories against an enemy that's going to be hard even to locate. We can only hope so.

At our son's wedding, Irish guests, New Yorkers, Southerners and Californians, with their different religions, beliefs, outlooks and heritages, came together to celebrate a joyous occasion which for that day surmounted the tragic events of the week. Was I imagining it or was there an extra warmth just because of these events? Something must have been going on because photographic evidence shows that your Observations writer (in a tux, no less) was dancing, along with everyone else, including some local gate-crashers who'd heard the music and come in, to a salsa band. There is an Irish toast, "Fad saol agat," which means "Long life to you." There is also a Jewish toast, "L'chaim," which means "To life." So, let's join the dance and let's get on with our lives.

Observations (and Ruminations) while Walking Around Sun City

Del Webb had a good idea when it provided every house in Sun City with an American flag. . . . Is the Rock Man, who sold many of those rocks studding Sun City front lawns, now doing the same in Lincoln Hills, or has he retired to some South Seas island, with no rocks? . . . There was a time when taking a walk in Sun City Roseville meant wending your way through work machines and pickup trucks and trying not to get mud on your shoes so as not to track up your new carpets. What happened to those little blue plastic booties we used to put on over our shoes so that our houses would remain immaculate? Maybe they've been collected and are now in Lincoln Hills. .

One of the added pleasures of taking a walk nowadays is getting away from the television and its all-day news broadcasts of the same thing over and over again as the "War on Terrorism" or "America Strikes Back" or whatever the latest is gets the O.J. Simpson/ Clinton scandal/ Gary Condit treatment. What next for all those talking heads who've derided American efforts in Afghanistan now after Kabul has been taken? I'm sure they'll come up with something. . . . What did all those local gardeners do before Sun City came along, or did they follow the crowd to Sun City? . . . . With all the trials and tribulations we had when we first moved in (I remember the Del Webb trucks going back and forth as homeowners called with one problem or another), that was still a memorable time, possibly because we were all in the same boat then. When we encountered a neighbor, or even a stranger, in the street, we compared notes and gave each other our best advice. Maybe the feeling was a little like that New Yorkers have had since September 11 .

The Canadian geese, a whole flock of them, are back on the golf course. I understand the golfers don't especially like them as they make a mess. But they are a sign that fall is here and that nature is following its regular course even during these trying times and that's reassuring. I notice they're staying off the green. One of the golf course assistants told me they put up a yellow rope on the green last year and the geese very politely stayed outside it so maybe these are the same geese and they remember from last year . . I haven't seen the heron or the egret who sometime hang out by the pond but they're probably around somewhere. I expect they'll return in due time to their usual routine of standing motionless for hours while the golfers and the rest of Sun City life go on around them. . .

Meanwhile, the holiday season has come as it does every year and Sun City custom demands that we throw ourselves into the usual round of Christmas lunches, dinners and parties, after which many of us will make our usual resolution to exercise regularly at the Fitness Center. . . The geese, heron and egret are presumably unaware of the unspecified terrorism threats we must be on the alert for, anthrax, the not-too-credible bridge warnings of our Governor, the anti-war protestors, the "experts" who say we're not persecuting the war vigorously enough and all the rest of it. Being aware of these things, I feel that this year there'll be more to our parties than eating and drinking, that there'll be a special meaning to friends and families getting together. After this, we'll be ready to face a new and uncertain year with vigilance (the price of liberty is eternal vigilance), with prudence but unafraid (the only thing we have to fear is fear itself), and with our flags still proudly waving.

2002 OBSERVATIONS

January 2002 Observations---on Last Year's Observations

What better way to spend time on a rainy December afternoon than to look through last year's Observations, especially if you're wondering what to say for the first Observations of 2002. Among last January's Observations, which looked back at the year 2000, was the big Y2K crisis that wasn't, the untimely death (at any time) of Peanuts creator Charles Schulz, summer gas prices of $2 per gallon, the advent of TV's first successful "reality" show, Survivors, and, definitely not least, the Florida election fiasco. Other year 2000 Observations touched on life's little annoyances, such as dealing with your HMO, the great California energy crisis, trying to cope with the ailments of aging (pills and more pills) and the events of September 11th and after.

Some observations on those Observations. Is there anything so out-of-date as last year's news? Does anyone besides possibly Al Gore still have any interest in the year 2000 presidential election? If so, September 11th extinguished it as it did many other things. As far as I know, the electoral college is still there and nobody is demanding that it be dismantled. There may be new voting machines next time but if there've been any front-page stories on this lately I've missed them. And even dangling chad jokes have disappeared.

Like the Y2K crisis, the energy crunch we were going to have last summer didn't happen. Don't ask me why not but, after our governor had signed expensive long-term contracts, cheap energy suddenly became available. Gas, which was supposed to go to $3 a gallon last summer, also suddenly became plentiful. But never fear, California still has its annual crisis, this time a state budget deficit of some $15 billion.

The TV show "Survivors", which might have been fun the first time around, spawned so many other "reality" shows, including sequels to itself, that we can only hope the glut eventually sinks them all. As for life's little annoyances, they keep piling up. Add. the phone ringing two or three times a day, then, after you've run to pick it up, no one answers. I'm told it's a computer dialing at random but with bad timing so that its message, whatever it is, doesn't coincide with the ringing. Maybe this year they'll fix the computer so you can at least tell it off and then hang up on it. By the way, if anyone wants to start a class-action suit on this, include me in. Also add those pop-up ads which are increasingly appearing on the computer. I began to notice this whenever I tried to get a sports result or financial news on Yahoo and instead kept getting the same ad for Flash 5.0. If anyone from Yahoo happens to read this, no, I don't want Flash 5.0. I've also stopped using Yahoo.

If you're like me, you keep on being surprised when you learn that some well-known person has passed on. This is especially true of sports and entertainment figures, who somehow seem forever young. I mean, I just saw Ingrid Bergman in a late movie last night and she looked the same as ever. I noted Charles Schulz's passing because his comic strip brought a daily smile to all of us. If I hadn't looked it up, I wouldn't have known that Imogene Coca died last year. She and Sid Caeser brought weekly laughs to millions of us in their ground-breaking Show of Shows in the 1950's. And now we have the Survivors, the Weakest Link (add that woman to life's little annoyances) and all the rest. By the way, can you imagine Sid and Imogene doing one of their satiric skits on any of these shows?

Finally, there's September 11th. If nothing else, it makes it a lot harder to foresee what's ahead in the coming year. Another terrorist attack of some kind and who knows what will result. But (as this is written) the Taliban has been all but driven out of Afghanistan and Bin Laden is being kept busy hiding in caves, this should put a crimp in terrorist activities and that's a good start for 2002.

February 2002 Observations

This "Observations" was my first dealing specifically with the problems encountered in retirement: either having too much time on your hands or, because you're scared of all that unoccupied time, getting involved in too many activities; and the inevitable health problems you have as you get older. I recommended having an unscheduled day every now and then and also getting a cat, both good suggestions, I think. I concluded by writing that retirement is a long-tem process that never ends, something I still think is very true.

Observations on Retirement

A short time ago I realized that I'd been retired for eleven years, longer than most jobs I had. I must admit I hadn't given too much thought to retirement when I left work. I just knew I'd worked long enough. I planned to sleep late (after years of getting up at 6:30 AM), have a leisurely breakfast and go from there. That, as a rookie retiree, was about it. So now, as a veteran retiree, what have I learned? Here, in no particular order, are some thoughts.

Most people, when they stop working, have to do something else. Otherwise, with all that extra time on their hands, they'll go nuts, not to mention driving their wives nuts. "Joe sits around the house all day doing nothing. He's always underfoot and I can't get anything done," is a typical wifely complaint. I suppose this explains why so many retirees (male) take to playing golf.

Women retirees don't have this problem because they go to lunches with other women retirees or, in a pinch, they can always spend the day shopping. At the other extreme from those guys who sit around the house all day are those retirees who tell you they're busier now than when they were working. They're the ones who are on all kinds of committees, volunteer for everything and anything, and rush around, carrying important-looking notebooks, to meetings every day. I suspect that most of these retirees got scared with all that free time when they stopped working, rushed into all the activities they could find to fill up every minute, and have never stopped rushing. Many of these busy retirees are women, who, in between their "work" activities also go to lunches and go shopping.

Every now and then, a retiree should have a completely unscheduled day when he (or she) doesn't have to be anywhere or do anything at any particular time. Every now and then, retirees should do something on the spur of the moment. Like, if you're a male retiree, saying to your wife, "Let's go out to lunch," or, "Let's hop over to Paris for the weekend."

Traveling when you're retired is a good thing to do, for the same reasons that it's good when you're still working. It's a change; it gets you out of your routine; you get to see new things and meet new people; you man even learn a thing or two. Traveling when you're retired is even better than when still working because you don't have to come back to your job and take care of all the things that have piled up while you've been away.

If you're a typical retiree, you're going to have health problems. No matter what your health problems, someone you know (probably everyone) has or has had the same problems, only infinitely worse, all of which you will hear about. From time to time when you're retired, perhaps especially when you're having health or other problems, you should recall, as you have your leisurely breakfast, all those years you had to get up at 6:30 AM and commute to work. And then had to commute back. This should make you feel better.

Retirees can go to movie matinees. This is good. It would be even better if they made better movies. Retirees can also go shopping during weekdays when stores are less crowded and drive during non-commute hours. Remind yourself of this and you'll feel better. When you're retired, or at any time, it's good to have a cat. By the time you're retired, you've seen that many of the things that troubled you in your younger years weren't that important after all. This is a good thing to keep in mind in your later years. Learning how to be a retiree is a long-term process that never ends. Keep working on it.

March 2002 Observations

In March, I looked at the outlook for the rest of the year. I again mentioned California's budget problems and observed, accurately, that the usual tricks would be used to make up the deficit. I also observed we were engaged in a funny kind of war (the term now used is "assymetrical") and asked if airport security would become such a hassle that people would give up traveling. No question airport security has become a hassle, worse than I imagined then. And some people have given up on airport travel. Maybe it will get even worse in the future.

As I write this, it's almost a month and a half into the year 2002. Many have said that after the events of last year, nothing in this country will be the same again. This is a little extreme but there's no question that many things have changed. So, peering into the clouded crystal ball (or is it my fading eyesight?), what's the outlook for this year?

The "war on terror," after the astonishing victory in Afghanistan, seems to be in a lull. Something has to take its place to feed the media's voracious appetite (CNN boasts that it's the 24/7 news channel) and that may be Enron. Already Washington's scandal-machinery is cranking up, with numerous congressional committees promising investigations. Look for the former federal prosecutors and other talking heads to come out of the woodwork and for the political parties to try to blame each other for the fiasco. By the way, when did 24/7 come into our language? Maybe it's a byproduct of television's determination to give us non-stop news, even when there isn't any.

California, of course, always has some kind of crisis on its hands, and, with the energy crisis still in abeyance, this year it will be the budget deficit of $12.5 billion or so. How did this happen? Well, when the money is coming in, you spend it all to make all the voting groups happy and get re-elected. When the money is gone, you scrounge from pension funds and whatever else is around and resort to the usual budget tricks to make up the difference.

As some have noted, this is a strange new kind of war we're in. For the most part, even though nothing is supposed to be the same, people go about their usual business. In fact, the government has officially declared that this is what we should do in fighting terrorism. But a few things are certainly changed. One is travel. Will the attempt to provide security at airports be such a hassle and will there be enough incidents of airport evacuation and passengers getting onto planes with weapons that a lot of people will give up on flying?

May 2002 Observations

Below another "Observations" on cruising, this time to the Mexican Riviera. I see I observed the confusion people seem to have about ship's elevators on cruises and this has been the case on all the cruises we've taken. I also observed that cruise passengers, after a few days of having every whim catered to, started to complain about things. It's common now that on every cruise we take the passengers recall how great cruising used to be and how badly things have fallen off. This of course doesn't stop them from signing up for the next cruise.

Observations Goes Cruising (Again)

My wife and I aren't cruisers in the same way that some other Sun Cityites are, ready to sail off at the drop of a hat or a drop in a fare. But over the course of our ten-plus retirement years, we've managed to go on a few cruises, the most recent being a sail along the west coast of Mexico, the Mexican Riviera. This has given us some perspective on the ins and outs of cruising, so herewith some Observations.

To get on our cruise ship, we flew from Sacramento to Los Angeles. This was our first flight since 9/11 and we weren't sure what to expect. But it was pretty much the same as before 9/11, a short flight after a long wait at the airport, except that our plane left and arrived on schedule.

I've noted before that the great surge in cruising is directly related to the increasing number of seniors in our population. This cruise was no exception. Most of the passengers would be at home in Sun City. In fact, I kept seeing people who I could have sworn I'd seen the week before in the Lodge.

The first day or two aboard, almost everyone raved about the ship: its facilities, the food, the shows, the service. By the third day, people began finding flaws: the choice of desserts was limited, the shore trip wasn't that interesting, the shows weren't up to the level of a Broadway production. Yes, we seniors have a tendency to be spoiled, or maybe we're just perfectionists.

This was the largest cruise ship we'd been on, carrying about 2,000 passengers. With that many aboard, I expected there to be some crowding, with lines to get into dinner or into shows but this never happened. I was constantly amazed that no matter where you went you didn't encounter a host of other people. These cruise lines know what they're doing in allocating space per passenger.

There must be something about ship elevators that's baffling to people. Almost every time I was on one of the elevators some group would get in not knowing what floor, or deck, they were on and whether they should be going up or down. Maybe it was the exotic names given to each deck that confused people. For example, our cabin, pardon me, stateroom, was on the Emerald deck, or E deck for short. It was easier thinking of E deck as the sixth floor.

We had a number of shore trips and there's nothing like coming off a cruise ship to a relatively poor country like Mexico to make you feel like a fat overstuffed American, partly because after a few days of eating those big cruise meals you are fat and overstuffed. I'm happy to say that we (especially the wives) did our best to give a boost to the local economy.

Of course you can't write about cruising without mentioning the cruise food. I've noted the big meals. In addition to the dining rooms with their elegant dinners, there was the non-stop buffet, the teas, the ice cream place and the pizza place. Almost every day after dinner, feeling satiated, we'd vow, "No mas." But somehow by the next day our appetites came back again. It must be all that fresh sea air.

Every cruise ship must have a cruise director and it's in the director's job description to be upbeat at all times. Our cruise director was so relentlessly cheerful that, if one (I use the British "one" as he was of that nationality) was cynical one would suspect that after the trip he went home and beat his wife and kids. Of course, I'm sure he did no such thing. As life for him was a perpetual cruise, he probably couldn't help but be cheerful all the time.

And let's face it, being on a cruise is great, a non-stop round of meals, shows, movies, games, relaxing in deck chairs, shore excursions to vary the tempo; what more could one (there's that word again) want. I think that by now we've more or less adjusted to leaving the cruise world for the real non-cruise world but with every passing day the cruise world is looking better. Fortunately, another cruise is coming up later in the year. Maybe this one will be perfect.

July 2002 Observations

My second "Observations" on life's little annoyances, now known as "LLA's" I see I complained about the ceaseless barrage of mail (and phone) requests for donations. This LLA hasn't changed, if anything it's gotten worse as more and more non-profit organizations seem to spring up every year. Once you've made one donation, you're in everyone's computer and the requests keep coming. There must be a better way.

Observations Takes Another Look at LLAs

Okay, it's good living here in Sun City and great to go cruising but it's time to get real and that means, you guessed it, taking another look at life's little annoyances (LLAs). How about the mail? It's just come, on my third trip to the mailbox, an LLA, and with it the daily complement of letters from non-profit organizations asking for donations. Now I'm sure most of these are for worthy causes: preserving the environment, saving wild animals, building homes for the poor. And for this reason, like many of you, I made my donations, in the spirit of the season, last December. So now every week I unfailingly get mail thanking me and then asking me for more. And lately, in addition to the letters, I've been getting calls, from earnest-sounding people, saying they need more and still more.

All right already. Give me a break. Even Bill Gates couldn't keep up with these constant pleas. And I've just paid my taxes. And besides, I'm starting to wonder, with all that money spent on those glossy-looking mailers, how much is really going to those worthy causes. A modest suggestion: once a donor has said, No, not now, take him (or her) out of your computer and save a lot of money. Then try again in, say, six months. And no more phone calls, please. That puts you in the class of those people who call you at dinnertime trying to sell you aluminum siding or worse.

Speaking of taxes (notice how I've worked this in), here is definitely a major LLA. I'm not speaking of having to pay a considerable part of your income to a government that spends it on $1,000 toilet seats or on studies to see if eating a lot makes you gain weight and other such items. Just filling out the forms and then doing everything necessary to send in your payment is enough to drive you up the wall. Take the form for figuring out your tax on capital gains. Let's put aside the question of why, if you were smart or lucky enough to make a gain on a stock or bond, you have to hand over part of it to Uncle Sam. The current capital gain tax is 20%. Fine. So you figure out your gain, take 20% of that, and that's your tax.

No, that would be too simple. You have to fill out Schedule D, both sides of it. This form contains such instructions as: Subtract line 22 from line 21. If zero or less, enter 0, and Enter the smaller of the amount on line 20 or $45,200 if married filing jointly or qualifying widow(er), $27,050 if single, $36,250 if head of household, or $22,600 if married filing separately. Then, once you have figured everything out (if you can) you have to send in your tax payment the proper way. This involves pasting the correct label on the correct envelope, filling out the payment form, putting your social security number in the proper places, etc., something like filling out all those forms and pasting in all those labels when you've "won" a million-dollar magazine contest. In fact, I wonder if the same people who make up those contest mailers are working for the IRS.

While there's some space left, we have to look at television, an unfailing source of LLAs. We've all gotten used to repeats, reality shows, abrupt program changes, the summer wasteland, still more repeats, still more reality shows. But things seem to be getting even worse. No sooner do you find a show you like and get used to watching it at a certain time on a certain day than it suddenly disappears. Sometimes it surfaces again at another time on another day. By this time, you and anyone else who's been watching, has completely forgotten the story line. A short time later, surprise, the show is cancelled. Then there's the ubiquitous CCN, news 24/7, whether there's any news or not. Also on the LLA list: any program in which two or more talking heads are supposedly debating an important topic; any program on which a former federal prosecutor appears; Chris Matthews.

Well, that's enough of LLAs for this month. Besides, the phone is ringing. It's probably someone thanking me for my last donation and asking for more.

August 2002 Observations

I see that in the "Observations" below, I noted that the unity our country achieved after 9/11 didn't last very long. I also note that our airport security was a joke. No changes since then except that things have gotten much worse. I also mention the Kings bitter loss to the Lakers. The Kings have never really recovered. I still think that with the good young players they now have there's hope for the future. At least I hope so.

Some Observations on Life's Disappointments

Although this Observations won't appear until August it's being written in the wake of the Kings bitter loss to the hated Lakers. This is certainly not the way the playoff series should have ended. Here were our Kings, on the verge of their greatest triumph after years of futility, playing against the puffed-up Lakers. If there was any justice in the world (as even Ralph Nader knew) the Kings would have prevailed. Instead, they fell just short.

It's the custom of sports writers, whether it's an NBA playoff, the World Series, the Super Bowl, even a major tennis tournament, to call the winners the greatest ever and to label the losers as soft (as in Chris Webber?), pretenders, chokers and, the worst, losers. Suddenly, the team or player who's made it to the finals "can't win the big one". What of the skills, the determination, the courage that have propelled them to the brink of a championship? These are forgotten. In everyone's disappointment, the losers are consigned to the ash heap.

Turning from sports to the larger world, another disappointment is the war on terror. Certainly Osoma Bin Laden should have been killed or captured by now. In a Hollywood script, the United States is attacked, we take over Afghanistan, we find Bin Laden, the terrorist threat is ended, the good guys have won, end of story. But Bin Laden eludes us, it seems the FBI couldn't catch a terrorist if they stumbled over one, our government issues ominous warnings of further attacks, and there's no end in sight. In our disappointment, congressional committees investigate, we demand to know who knew what when, someone must be to blame.

I think it's fair to say that there's a general disappointment with our government. After September 11th, the country pulled together behind the President; Democrats and Republicans even embraced each other on the Capitol steps. This unity didn't last very long. The economic incentive plan died, a stillbirth. As anyone who's taken an airplane trip lately knows, the so-called security measures won't stop any determined professional terrorist, or even some insane amateur.

If we're disappointed with our government, what about our great free enterprise system? It turns out that leading corporations, aided and abetted by leading accounting firms, have been cooking their books and scamming the public. Our largest brokerage house seems to have been touting stocks which they privately considered "dogs." The economy is still iffy and we know which way the stock market has been going, down, down, down.

It's evident that life is full of disappointments. I know I'm disappointed every day when the mail comes and consists only of ads and requests for money, not that big prize or great news I'm waiting for. In sports, the consolation is that there's always the next season or the next big tournament. The Kings, needless to say, aren't losers. They just happened to lose the conference final series, and in a seventh-game overtime at that. Next year they should be even better (they'd better re-sign Mike Bibby) and maybe they'll go all the way.

In the wider world, all may not lost either. The FBI is reorganizing. They're even talking to the CIA. We might eventually have a new agency to coordinate anti-terrorist activities.

CEO's are resigning by the score. Merrill Lynch actually apologized to its clients. Stocks can't keep going down forever, can they?

So if it's possible that big business and even our government can learn something from disappointments maybe we can, too. And if not maybe we can shake them off, be they with sports teams, our stocks, our children, ourselves, and get beyond them. Hope springs eternal. Maybe the next mail delivery will contain something great. Next season the Kings may take that final step. (But be sure to re-sign Bibby).

September 2002 Observations

Another "Observations" on travel, this time to Eastern Europe. I see that I wrote a lot about the discomforts of air transport, and this was even while airlines still served meals, bad though they were, and didn't yet charge for luggage.

Over the summer my wife and I made our first trip to Eastern Europe, spending a few days each in Prague (Praha to the locals) and Budapest (pronounced Budapesht). Before getting to these cities we of course had to endure the ordeal by flying. As the hub city of our airline was Chicago, this meant going from Sacramento to Chicago, then Chicago to Frankfurt, then Frankfurt to Prague. It was appropriate that our Prague hotel was located right next to a cemetery because by the time we got there we were dead on arrival.

It goes without saying that our airlines had decided legroom for their passengers was unnecessary, and that the airplane food was made of wood and cardboard. This has become standard for air travel nowadays and, short of a consumer revolution with the public saying, "I'm not taking this any more," nothing much can be done about it. But the 24-hour long travel day allowed plenty of time to consider what might be done about two of the worst problems in flying: how to extract yourself from your seat with a trayful of half-eaten (or uneaten) airline food in your way and then how to navigate your way to the facilities.

To begin with, you can barely move in your seat with the tray up. When a meal (so-called) is served and your tray is down you are really pinned in. If the passenger in front of your has set back his seat, something almost guaranteed to happen, you are just about impaled by your tray. Then, having eaten what you can stomach you want to use the facility. Needless to say, the airline servers, having delivered the meals, have mysteriously disappeared. So you must somehow get rid of the things on your tray and then somehow edge your way out into the aisle, at which point you discover where the servers are, in the aisle with a huge cart blocking your way.

The solution to this problem came to me when for the third time we were told about the oxygen masks dropping from the plane's ceiling in case of the cabin losing pressure. If something can be dropped down, then why can't things be lifted up. In my scheme, patent pending, an arm descends, plucks up your discards, then puts them on a conveyer belt which delivers them to the kitchen. If the airlines can design planes with just enough room to allow passengers to squeeze into their seats and not an inch more, designing such a retrieval system should be simple enough. There remains the problem of those huge carts invariably blocking your way, like trucks or motor homes on the highway. Since passing lanes don't seem practical. in an airplane the best solution would be to have narrower carts (and thinner servers), thus allowing passengers to get past.

Now that this has been taken care of, some observations on Eastern Europe. Being behind the times, this was the trip we finally discovered ATMs. Both Prague and Budapest have ATMs which give their instructions in English so you just follow them and, voila, out comes the local currency. Beats travelers checks and trying to decide which change place offers the best rates. Both cities have subways which are easy to use and will take you anywhere. Our Prague hotel by the cemetery was six stops from downtown so we took it daily, getting tickets from the concierge. We were told to get our tickets stamped (by inserting in a machine) and this was good advice as a couple in our group who failed to do this were caught and had to pay a fine.

We were also told to watch out for pickpockets and this too was good advice as someone had his wallet plucked from his fanny pack. This was the only such incident our group had so the only advice I can offer is to be alert, carry as little as possible, have backups for whatever you carry and hope the pickpockets don't target you. In Prague, we got our subway tickets from our hotel. In Budapest, we had to get them from a machine, but this was no problem as the machine, like an ATM, spoke English and the instructions were equally easy to follow.

Trying to regain our equilibrium after our horrible flights, my wife and I spent a goodly amount of time café-sitting. In Prague, we'd recommend trying the apple strudel, which was better even than that in Vienna. In both Prague and Budapest, as an alternative to the local drink, Coca Cola, try the iced coffee, served with both whipped and ice cream. In Prague, our guide suggested going to the Black Light theater and I'd pass this on to readers. The theater is conveniently located just off Old Town Square, is inexpensive and there's no talking so you don't have to know Czech. In Pest, it's pleasant to dine in one of the many outdoor places along the Danube, especially at night, when you can see the lights of the castle on the hill in Buda across the river as well as the lights of the bridges.

Both cities have buildings going back to early centuries, with interesting architecture, castles up on hills and churches of all kinds, plus historic synagogues. They are amazingly clean and, unlike Italy, which we visited the previous summer, you can cross streets without risking your life. The people are well-dressed and, at least to a tourist's eye, seem to be doing well. Streets are busy, cafes filled and stores were doing a brisk business You can hear American jazz everywhere and the young people dress and look like Americans. In fact, some of the young people were Americans; Eastern Europe is definitely on the backpack-through-Europe, circuit. So perhaps you'll want to visit there soon, before all the sidewalk cafes are taken over by Starbucks (there's already one in Vienna). Don't wait until my suggestions for improving air travel are put into effect.

October 2002 Observations---on Life's Little Joys

As faithful Observations readers know, from time to time I've commented on what I've called life's little annoyances (LLAs), those things which we all come up against as we go through our day-to-day activities. LLAs include those computerized calls everyone gets two or three times daily, always at inconvenient times; the automated phone systems that have replaced human beings; the credit card offers and requests for donations which make up the bulk of our mail; the spam which makes up most of our e-mail; TV news, TV commercials, TV shows, HMOs and so on and on.

My wife, who has a sunnier disposition than me, has suggested that, however satisfying it is to vent about LLAs, I should balance this out somewhat by having an Observations about life's little joys, LLJs. So here is a sampling of LLJs (most of them my wife's suggestions).

You're on your way to go shopping and someone slows down to let you change lanes. No one tailgates you. You spot a great parking spot and nobody beats you to it. In the store, you find just what you were looking for and what's more it's on sale. I'll add: you find a sales counter with no line and a sales clerk who actually knows what she (or he) is doing.

The phone rings and it's not a computer or a hang-up call but someone you know (and want to hear from). That someone asks if you want to go out to lunch. At lunch, you find some new great dish. You come home, weigh yourself and you haven't gained anything. (This allows you to go out to lunch again later in the week).

Something good, among all the junk, comes in the mail. Maybe it's a card or letter from an old friend you haven't heard from in a while. Maybe it's a card from your son or daughter on your birthday. Even better, the son or daughter sends a bouquet of flowers. For wives, your husband takes you out to dinner. The servers all come over and serenade you with their version of Happy Birthday. (Well, I don't know about that one). For husbands, your wife cooks your favorite meal and you don't have to go out.

The library calls and tells you that book you reserved months ago and have forgotten about has finally come in. You go to get the book and find another one, the latest by your favorite author you hadn't known was out yet. While you're home reading one of these books, having completely forgotten about preparing dinner, your husband says, Let's get some take-out.

Some other LLJs: planning a trip. Going on the trip. Returning from the trip and finding everything is okay---your plants haven't dried up, your cat remembers you, your appliances still work, the morning paper has resumed delivery. Afterwards, looking at pictures you took of the trip I'll add: having some money left after the trip. After one too many trips, staying at home.

While at home: your neighbor brings over some fresh tomatoes. You solve the New York Times crossword puzzle. You have nothing to do the rest of the day. Your cat comes over and sits on your lap. (Dog lovers can supply their own canine LLJs.)

As I read through these LLJs it strikes me that many are the opposite of LLAs. Usually, someone does tailgate you. Usually, someone darts in ahead of you to get that great parking space. Usually, that thing you're shopping for is no longer in stock or they don't have your size.

And so on. So I'll conclude by hoping that for you the LLJs balance out the LLAs. As for me, the LLJs I want are: to have a day without a hangup phone call, to call some company and get a human being and to go to my HMO and see my doctor immediately. These are probably not LLJs but more like LLMs, life's little miracles.

November 2002 Observations

A little over a year ago I did an Observations asking pertinent, or possibly impertinent, questions regarding events of that time. One of the questions was: would Governor Gray Davis make a run for president on the claim that he'd solved the California energy crisis he'd at least in part helped create? When this Observations appears, it will be the beginning of November and Election Day will be just around the corner. Davis hasn't had the chance to run for president yet but he is running for re-election as governor against Republican Bill Simon, raising the question: how come our choice for governor comes down to these two guys? And how many times in the last few years in how many elections have we asked ourselves the same question?

Okay, enough politics for now, the question that comes up as I drive around Roseville and adjoining areas is: who are the people buying all of those not inexpensive houses that are going up everywhere? Are they more people from the Bay Area who are selling their even more expensive houses and moving here? I'd thought that by now everyone from down there who wanted to move up here had already done so. But maybe not? If not more Bay Area emigres, then who?

A related question: who are the people (besides Sun City residents) who are packing all of the new restaurants in the Roseville area? I thought we were in an economic slump but apparently this doesn't apply when it comes to eating out. Another question: why do parents insist on bringing young and noisy children, including babies, to fancy restaurants and then spend the entire meal trying, usually in vain, to keep them quiet? Maybe they are feeling the economic slump so they're saving money by not hiring baby-sitters.

Another question that comes up while driving around (and again on a matter I've touched on before here): what is all this new road construction? This question arose when I found that Roseville Parkway had been blocked off and later when I found that two lanes of

Foothills Boulevard had been closed. So when is construction on our local roads going to be completed? I think I know the answer to that one: not in our lifetime.

A couple of questions arising from the start of a new television season. The critics have been falling all over themselves praising the crime family series, "The Sopranos." I'll admit that having the father's occupation being "gang boss and killer" rather than sports writer or architect or advertising exec lends the show a little piquancy and it is kind of fun to guess which cast member will be the next to be "whacked." But is the show really that good and when you come down to it isn't "The Sopranos", like all those other gangster tv's and films, a glorification of someone who, despite his anxieties and endearing ways, is essentially a guy who extorts money from the public and who, every few episodes, kills people?

The show which is at the opposite extreme from "The Sopranos" and which has been almost as critically acclaimed is of course, "The West Wing." It's a good show but am I the only one who finds many of the fictional White House staff glib and at least a touch arrogant? Of course, this could be true of real White House staffers and so maybe the show's writers are just showing it like it is.

This brings us back to politics and to another one of my questions from a year ago: wouldn't President Bush, having been deemed by the media as not too bright, benefit when he did do something good? The question was posed before 9/11 and maybe the almost universal accolades given Bush's decisive actions right after that event were to some extent due to the low expectations many had of him (Strangely enough, the fictional Republican presidential candidate's lack of smarts has become a "West Wing" story line.)

Speaking of 9/11 leads to a final question: what's happened to that spirit of unity that we had after that date? I suppose it was asking too much that it persist. So, how do we rekindle it? I'd say that's asking what they used to call the $64,000 question.

December 2002 Observations

Another "Observations" below dealing with retirement issues, this time on how retirement life has become so complex we ask, "Where is all that free time I thought I'd have when I quit working?" I think the answer is a combination of things. As we get older, we slow down. There are matters of health to be dealt with: doctor and dentist appointments, prescriptions to fill, tests to take. All those difficult choices: which phone service to take; what credit card offers to consider; which computers to buy; what cruises to go on. Those afternoon naps (and other times when we just doze off. *Whatever the reasons, I'm sure I'm not alone in thinking, how did I find the time to do all these things when I was working?*

In my early days as a retiree I thought in all innocence that life would get much simpler. After all, I didn't have a job, with all of its demands and tensions, to worry about any more. I didn't have a daily commute. I'd have all that free time. I could play all the tennis I wanted. We'd be able to travel. Little did I know how wrong I was. Instead of getting simpler, life has become more and more complex.

Of course, some of this complexity has to do with simply getting older. At one time when I played tennis I'd just pick up my racket and go. Now preparing for tennis is a time-consuming ritual: anti-inflammation pills for those arthritic joints, a support for my tendonitis-afflicted wrist, sun block to ward off skin cancers, a check to see that I have my water bottle (can't get dehydrated) and, finally, making sure I have my racket (with all those other things to remember, I could very well forget this).

Travel too has gotten more complicated. No longer can we throw a few things into a suitcase and take off. There are those pills we have to take for our various ailments, more pills to ward off cold germs from fellow tourists, lightweight clothes in case it's hot, heavier clothes in case it gets cold, money belts to thwart pickpockets, the list seems endless. No wonder we have to spend a week packing.

Other things making life more complex have to do with the times we live in. Take credit cards. Sometime in the past, I don't know how far back, I got a credit card. I could charge things and hope I could meet the payments. Simple enough. Now every day I'm bombarded by solicitations for different credit cards. The question is: of all these cards, with all of their various deals, which to choose? Then, after finally choosing a card, that company bombards you with constant offers to upgrade. Is it worth paying the extra money for some extra benefits? I suppose people who aren't retired get all of this credit card stuff, too, but they're probably too busy to care and throw all of it away. As retirees, it's up to us to carefully consider everything and make the best and most economical choice. It's all very complex.

Equally complex, not too say confusing, are the millions of telephone service options to consider. It used to be simple. The telephone company was the telephone company. You got a phone and paid your bill or you'd be cut off. Nowadays, there are cell phones, cordless phones, digital phones, answering machines, phone-ID, phone-blocking, I couldn't begin to catalogue all of the things available to today's baffled consumer. Then, after you've gotten a phone service, the only thing you get are those hang-up computer calls.

Another thing we retirees have to spend days considering are all of the travel bargains, cruises, safaris and other excursions which come in every mail. When I was working, it was simple. We didn't go on many vacations and those we did go on were for the kids. Now we have to decide for ourselves and again it's pretty complex. Then there's the matter of choosing which HMO or other medical system to use. In the very old days, you'd have a doctor down the street and go to him. If you had a really bad problem, some friend would be sure to recommend a "specialist," meaning that he had a fancier office and charged more money. Now, with all of the great medical advances we have, we try to find some system where we might possibly get in to see a doctor within six months.

There's also the matter of long-term care. Should we have insurance and pay quite a bit of money now just in case or take our chances and then possibly be faced with exorbitant nursing home bills in the future? Of course, there's the final matter: what do we do about leaving this world? Burial? How? Where? How expensive? Cremation? Where to scatter the ashes? With all of the choices, this too has become complex. But, come to think of it, I'll be gone then so, should I really worry about all of this stuff? Think I'll look through all that travel material, pick one, then go on a cruise and forget everything else. That'll be keeping it simple.

2003 OBSERVATIONS

January 2003 Observations

Another "Observations" on the year past, this time the year 2002. I observed the decline in the economy, the job cuts and the slumping stock market. Sounds like the year 2008 or the year 2009 (although the stock market did recover in 2009). Guess things don't change too much. I wrote that people would be resilient enough to handle all these bad things. I think that, despite everything, this is still true today.

Observations on the Year Past

This piece about the year 2002 is being written in early December so some event such as a terrorist attack or even another sniper spree, if it happens before the year ends, will change the complexion of the past 12 months. Still, I think it's fair to say even now that 2002, the year following 9/11/01, was not one of our better times. There was of course the decline in the economy, job cuts and a slumping stock market. But almost every aspect of life had its low points, especially, it seems, for those of us who dwell in California.

In politics. we had the choice of Gray Davis or Bill Simon as governor for the next four years, certainly a low point even for this state. And we're already being told that our budget deficit will be getting worse. Let's hope that the next earthquake won't be the really big one.

In sports, the low point for us Kings' fans was the fluke field goal that Robert Horry made in the playoffs against the hated Lakers and that has enabled Shaqueille O'Neill to strut ever since. Fans of the Raiders, 49ers, A's and 49ers didn't fare much better. The 49ers lost in the playoffs. Worse, the Raiders lost in the playoffs when a fumble by New England quarterback Tom Brady was ruled not to be a fumble. The A's were upset in the playoffs. Worse, the Giants lost the World Series in the 7th game after being ahead three games to two.

In entertainment, movies once again hit a new low. The exception was My Big Fat Greek Wedding, which our Sacramento Bee film critic gave one and a half stars, thereby reaching a personal low point for himself. It goes without saying that television, which manages to get worse every year, again hit a new low in 2002, with more and more network time taken up by shows like "The Bachelor," "The Fear Factor," and other so-called "reality" shows.

Travel got more difficult in 2002. Enough has been written about this so I need not go into details except to note that on our last flights to the East and back the "lunch" and "dinner" both ways were identical "bistro" bags containing an inedible "chicken" sandwich.

Finally, on the terrorist front, while 2002 saw nothing like WTC attack, the determination that Osama Bin Laden was still alive and the warning of a "spectacular" attack, were not exactly high points.

The flights to the East mentioned above were to New York City. Having grown up there, I'd never before stayed at a hotel in midtown Manhattan. No, that visit wasn't a low point of the year for us. I mention the trip because, just a little over a year after 9/11/02, our hotel was filled with tourists, the theaters were doing a good business, the restaurants were packed, the streets were filled people all in a hurry to get somewhere. In short, the city was back in business. What this shows is that people have an amazing resiliency. So, despite all the low points I've enumerated, we begin the new year hoping, as always, that the world will get better. And this is taking into account the Iraqi situation, war or no war.

Next time, the Kings, 49ers, A's and Giants will go all the way. Movies and TV will miraculously get better. The airline industry will recover. This will fuel a general economic recovery. The stock market will go up, or at least stop going down. California will cope with its deficit. Maybe we'll even get Osama. It's the beginning of the year so anything is possible. And whatever happens, we'll be resilient enough to handle it.

February 2003 Observations

Another "Observations" on cruising, in which I call it a brief escape from the real world. I quote one of the cruise ship's comedians as saying, "You know you're not on a cruise any more when you drop a towel and it's not picked up." This about sums it up.

Observations on Travel and Cruising (Again)

In January, my wife Beverly (see Favorite Restaurants) and I had a wedding to go to in Florida and as that's usually a dreary month in these parts we decided to take a Caribbean cruise afterwards. Before looking at the cruise, for any readers who haven't traveled by plane yet this year, some encouraging news. With airlines either already in bankruptcy or heading there and with the new requirement that onboard airplane luggage had to be screened, I naturally expected the worse. So I was pleasantly surprised that there was no delay either at the Sacramento Airport, where we checked in at curbside, or at the Orlando airport returning from our Caribbean cruise. Airline people, who I'd read were becoming mean and surly because of job stress, were courteous and efficient. Since our last trip on it, the airline had contrived to add a little more legroom. In Orlando, after the cruise ship had dumped us off early even though our flight didn't leave until after three, the ticket people even found an earlier flight to put us on.

This doesn't mean that air travel still isn't a test of patience and endurance. Before reaching the ticket desk in Orlando, we had to wait on a long line with other people going home from cruises or from Disney World. Airline food, if there is any, is still terrible. And it's still annoying that airport screeners seem to have a rule that they should search the carry-ons of senior citizens. But, as we senior citizens want to be treated like anyone else, I guess I shouldn't complain and who's to say that seniors aren't more likely than nuns and mothers with babies to be terrorists. Oh, yes, as has been the case the last couple of years, all of our flights were on schedule. Maybe the threat of bankruptcy has done something to make airlines fly on time.

So much for the necessary evil of flying. Now, on to the cruise. Food, drink, shows, games, gambling, food, the Captain's reception, the high tea, bingo, the formal dinners, more food. I seem to be mentioning food. Let's face it, the highlight of the day for most cruise passengers, or cruisers, is the five-course dinner. Then there are the many-course breakfasts and lunches, the almost never-ending buffet, the pizza, hot dogs and hamburgers, the midnight desserts. There isn't a moment when food isn't available and, when food is available, the people aboard ship will eat it. After all, they've already paid for it, haven't they? I'm not saying that going on a cruise turns us all into gluttons but I must note that I haven't seen as many large people in one place since, well, since our last cruise. With all the current furor about America's obesity, It's a wonder that some lawyer hasn't gotten all these large people together to file a class-action suit against the cruise lines for making them fat.

But cruisers aren't usually in a litigating mood because cruising is a brief escape from the real world. So we can eat all we want (vacation calories don't count; you've heard that before), spend our time going to shows, which, while not exactly of Broadway caliber, are certainly entertaining enough for cruising, sit in lounges where stewards are always alert to bring us drinks and play bingo to our heart's content while our cabins are kept in perfect order by still more stewards. In fact, one of the show comedians said that you know when you're not cruising any more when you drop a towel on the floor and it's not picked up.

In our case, returning to reality came with a jolt as, passing Cape Canaveral on the way to the Orlando airport, we saw people lining the highway watching for the return of the shuttle, then in the airport we learned of the shuttle's tragic end. Then, back in California, there was the state financial crisis, the budget cuts and new taxes, the possible increased Sun City dues, and of course Iraq. But at least we don't have to face any more five-course dinners.

April 2003 Observations---on Taxes & Other Taxing Matters

This Observations, which will appear around April 1st, is being written in between doing my taxes in March, so it's being done before the Iraqi War started and while TV is busy showing thousands of protesters marching in the streets. Since the 1960's, we've become accustomed to such protests and, in California especially, I'm sure a few thousand people can be rustled up to protest just about anything on a moment's notice. But, I'm not aware of masses of senior citizens taking to the streets to protest government unfairness or to demand senior rights.

Every year when I do my taxes I'm annoyed at the government for taxing 85 percent of my social security benefits (readers may recall that it was increased from 50 to 85 percent some years ago on the grounds that the government desperately needed more money and has remained there even when we had a surplus). I suppose I dislike this tax, no matter what the percent, because after spending many, many years paying into social security now I have to pay a tax on what is at least in part my money.

Then there are medical and dental expenses. True, there's a tax deduction for these but not if over 7.5 percent of your gross income. This means that if your gross income is $50,000 your expenses aren't deductible unless over $3,750, in which case your health insurance is probably not too great or, worse, you have no insurance at all. And many health plans, whatever else they cover, don't pay for prescription drugs. The government, both Republicans and Democrats, has talked about doing something about this for I don't know how many years but nothing has been done. Then there's dental care, which, like prescription drugs, becomes more and more expensive as we get older. I don't know of anyone who's completely covered for dental expenses and things like root canals and bridges can run into the thousands.

Still another area where the government doesn't do much for its senior citizens is long-term care. I know of many people in Sun City who have to take care of parents or spouses in need of such care and here the average person is on his (or her) own. The choices seem to be: go broke and then qualify for Medi-Cal, pay for some kind of long-term care insurance, not cheap, or take your chances with paying nursing home or home health care costs, definitely not cheap. There must be a better way.

I've never been a fan of protests, especially by ungrateful foreigners whose countries we've saved or by ungrateful citizens who deem that anything our country does must be bad. But, hey, if the way to get noticed and be all over television is to take to the streets, maybe we seniors should consider it. Okay, I'm not completely serious (I tend to have a lot of wild notions every year when doing taxes) but eventually, who knows? Meanwhile, I'll check on our American flag so it'll be ready to hoist as soon as we take on Iraq because no matter what faults our government has it's still ours Taxes or not, as people used to say after 9/11, God bless America.

May 2003 Observations

The "Observations" below notes the start of the Iraq war (George W's one).and observes that it was almost over. We had no trouble getting into Iraq; the problem, as we know now, was getting out.

I ended last month's Observations by saying I was going to check on our American flag to be sure it was ready to hoist as soon as we took on Iraq. The flag has duly been put out, as have many others in Sun City. For this month, I was ready to offer my armchair critique of the war as Cpl. Martin Green, Seventh Army (ret.). This idea had to be discarded because as of this writing (April 12) the war seems to be just about over without benefit of my advice (and despite the criticisms of a number of armchair generals, ret.). In any case, with all the millions of words about the war already written elsewhere, not to mention the 24/7, or is it 7/24, coverage on television, I've decided to put Iraq aside for a while and, somehow taking off from putting out the flag, try to find a few things in everyday non-Iraq life worthy of saluting.

Since I start off the day by getting the morning newspaper, I'd like to salute first whoever it is that chose to continue running Peanuts (and of course a salute to the memory of Charles Schultz), thereby ensuring a smile to start the day. I'd also like to salute Lynn Johnston, the lady who created the comic strip For Better or for Worse, which doesn't have sex or violence, doesn't grind any political axe, but simply follows the lives of an ordinary family, with all of the ups and downs everyone has experienced, and day in and day out manages to do it in a humorous way. There's another smile to start the day.

Turning to the sports page, and since the NBA playoffs are about to begin, here's a salute to the Sacramento Kings organization. Yes, the Kings were for more years than we fans like to remember one of the worst teams in the league. The current organization has turned it into one of the best. If there's any justice at all, this will be the year in which they prove they are the very best. As long as we're at it, a salute to the Kings' players, none of whom, to my knowledge, has beaten up his wife or girl friend, been involved with drugs or refers to himself in the third person.

Before leaving the morning paper, a non-salute, or rebuke, for imbedding the Scene section, which contains the important comic strips, TV listings and crossword puzzles, in millions of ads so that every day it requires a major search mission to discover it?

Okay, I said I'd put Iraq aside for a while but I have to make one observation, that a considerable segment of our media, in addition to the aforementioned armchair generals, ret., seems ready to jump all over our armed forces at the slightest hint that things aren't going 100 percent successfully. This happened when there was a two or three day pause before the attack on Baghdad. Now it's happening because the Iraqis, after years of repression, are (gasp!)

actually looting things. I could offer my advice on controlling unruly crowds on the basis of my two years experience as president of the New Yorkers club but I suspect that by the time this appears the looting will have subsided and, of course, something else will have come up, like where is Saddam or how come Baghdad doesn't have television yet.

Well, like the past month, this has been a pretty choppy Observations, some salutes, some rebukes. I'd like to end on an upbeat note by saluting the men and women who've been doing the actual fighting in Iraq. I'll also note that one morning last week the Scene wasn't hidden away in wads of advertising, so maybe there's hope even for our media. And here's a hope that by now, around May 1, the Iraqi operation is all over.

June 2003 Observations on Weddings & Funerals

Some years ago a film called Four Weddings and a Funeral appeared. It was, as I recall, a critical and box-office success and, aside from inflicting the actor Hugh Grant on an unsuspecting public, a pretty good movie. Part of its success was, I think, that weddings and funerals strike a response in us all as ceremonies marking important stages of life. Weddings signify the beginning of a new phase for a (usually) young couple, a commitment and a step toward maturity. Funerals of course mark the ending of a life.

All of this is by way of introducing the subject of this month's Observations, which, as you've guessed, is Weddings and Funerals, and is probably not even necessary except that I wanted to get in that crack about Hugh Grant. The subject comes up because over the past few months, we (my wife Beverly and myself) have been to several weddings as various family members get married and anticipate going to still another wedding (this an Irish one) later this year. We have also, regrettably, gone to two funerals in the past year, both of friends residing in Sun City.

Weddings, especially those of your own children, are happy occasions. (Now they definitely can't come back to live with you. Just joking, of course). The stars of the occasion are the wedding couple. The bride, no matter what the trials and tribulations of the wedding planning have been, is always glowing now that the big day has finally come. The groom, who probably has had as little to do with the planning as possible, always has a kind of sappy smile on his face. The bridesmaids, no matter how they look in ordinary life, are always beautiful. Even the male members of the wedding party, all dressed up in their tuxes, look good.

When my son married, I was a major supporting actor, a member of the wedding party. At the other two weddings, I was merely a minor actor, almost an extra, the "uncle from California." Regardless of the wedding, and they were all completely different from each other, everyone shared in the good feeling engendered from the obvious joy of the bride and groom and joined in wishing them more happiness for the future. As a senior coming to the end of the line (but not too soon, I hope), I was glad to participate in this new beginning. For at beginnings, the slate is clean, there is hope and optimism and only good things lie ahead.

Funerals, in contrast to weddings, can be depressing events, which is why I don't plan to attend my own. But I think we all recognize them as necessary, if only to give family and friends a formal setting for their grief and whatever other feelings they may have. Funerals also offer a venue for the summing up of a life. It's a time to recall that the person you've come to pay your last respects to was not always, and just, a grandfather, a World War II veteran, a member of this or that club. He was also a schoolboy, a hopeful teenager, a young man starting his first job, and ,yes, a happy bridegroom embarking on the next stage of his life.

So what do we conclude from all this? Lead the kind of life that you'd like to have summed up at your funeral. Meanwhile, attend all the weddings you can. You'll come away feeling good and maybe those good feelings will postpone your funeral.

July 2003 Observations

I'd long thought that certain inanimate objects are hostile to mankind, a good example being those coat hangers that always get intertwined with each other. I named the computer as the main offender in our house so must have been having problems with it at that time. My computer has been behaving itself lately but you never know. A more recent inanimate object we've taken into our house is the cell phone and I'm not too sure of its intentions.

Observations on Inanimate Objects

I recently finished a novel, "Prey," by Michael Crichton, a writer famous for anticipating scientific breakthroughs and their effects on society, usual pretty dire (he's also the author of "Jurassic Park.") The scientific breakthrough explored in "Prey," (the title warns that it's not going to benefit mankind) is that of nanotechnology, which is the creation of miniature machines, I mean really little, like a million will fit into a drop of water. These little machines, created to form a swarm, like many bees swarming together, able to fly overhead and act as spy cameras (the project is financed by the military, of course) get out of control and swarm together all right but not to take pictures. Their intention seems to be to attack the people (the prey) who created them and either take over their bodies or eat them.

Crichton's message is that when man creates such things we should proceed with caution, something that the author of "Frankenstein" (Mary Shelley) would undoubtedly agree with. But we who struggle with them daily know that so-called inanimate objects have always had agendas of their own, usually inimical to human beings, and they don't have to be tiny objects, they can be of normal size.

My own candidate for most annoying inanimate objects are clothes hangers. You can hang up your clothes as neatly as possible at night but when you go to get them in the morning the hangers have somehow become intertwined with each other and you have to untangle them to get your clothes for the day. What do these clothes hangers do overnight? Do they say, "I'm tired of hanging around here, let's get together and give those humans something to wrestle with"?

Then there are belts. No matter how carefully you hang up a belt, when you want to use it, it's managed to slip off its hanger or hook or whatever and fallen to the floor, in a dark corner. Of course, if it's been put on a clothes hanger, the hanger is an accomplice. Towels are another example of objects that, no matter how carefully hung up, always find their way to the floor.

Other inanimate objects that have a mind of their own, usually not inclined to cooperate with the humans who want to use them, are can openers, microwaves, dishwashers, air conditioners, VCRs and vacuum cleaners. My wife Beverly's list of uncooperative objects includes pencils, flashlights, scissors and bookmarks. No matter where you put these so that they'll be handy when needed, they have a habit of vanishing. The phone rings, you have to make a note of some important information, you reach for the pencil you placed by the phone and it's gone. There's a power outage. You grope your way to the drawer where you've put the flashlight for just such an emergency and it's mysteriously not there. The same with scissors and bookmarks. Where do these objects go? They must be around someplace. Often, when you're looking for something else, you'll find a missing object and be baffled as to how it got there. You know those mysterious sounds our Sun City homes make at night. Maybe these are all the inanimate objects moving to their hiding places.

But of course the number one culprit among uncooperative objects is the computer. My theory is that computers, like wives, get tired of being taken for granted and want to show their presumed owners what life is like if they're not there. So every now and then, no matter what you're doing on the computer, you get the message, "You have performed an illegal operation and are being shut down." At other times, like a wife who stops talking to you, the computer will suddenly freeze up and won't unfreeze no matter what you do. The only solution, usually, is to close down the computer, wait for a decent interval, then try for a fresh start. Roses might also help.

In Michael Crichton's book, the tiny inanimate particles gain power by swarming together. This can have scary consequences. We have already seen how coat hangers and belts can collude. My advice: keep a close eye on your inanimate objects. Never let your can opener, dishwasher or VCR get together with your computer. If they ever do, you're in real trouble.

August 2003 Observations

Another "Observations" below on the good old days, in this instance the good old radio days. Our kids and certainly our grandkids will find it hard to believe that our chief means of home entertainment was the radio. I retain a fondness for those old radio shows and don't think I'll ever have the same feeling about even the few good television shows we've had.

The other day one of the crossword clues involved the old radio show Fibber McGee and Molly. The only thing I remember about this show is that when Fibber McGee opened his closet everything came flying out (via radio sound effects), something like my own closet. But it did trigger recollections of all those other old radio shows we used to listen to when we were kids.

The first one that comes to my mind is Jack Armstrong, All-American boy, who, as I remember it, went to Hudson High. Jack didn't smoke, do drugs, listen to rock music or engage in any of the typical activities of today's teenagers. He just went around doing good things and saving people. How things have changed.

Another somewhat older hero was the Lone Ranger, who galloped onto the screen . . . no, this was radio . . . who galloped in our imaginations to the accompaniment of the hoof beats, created by the sound effects man, of his mighty horse Silver, and, probably the one piece of classical music we knew, the William Tell Overture. The Lone Ranger of course was accompanied by his faithful Indian companion Tonto and we all know that his famous phrase "Kimo Sabe" means "Watch you step, paleface." No, that would be what it meant if the Lone Ranger was riding today.

The Green Hornet also came with the sound of music, was it the "Flight of the Bumblebee"? And he too had his faithful companion, his valet Kato. By the way, when he was not being the Green Hornet, this hero was Britt Reede, editor of the Illustrated Press, or am I thinking of Steve Wilson, as portrayed by none other than Edward G. Robinson. Anyway, can we imagine any of today's media people being a superhero?

The Shadow was portrayed by another illustrious actor, none other than the young Orson Welles, who was much thinner then and so was better able to make himself invisible by clouding the minds of men. And the Shadow, even back in those innocent days, knew what evil lurked in the hearts of men. Like the Lone Ranger and the Green Hornet, the Shadow had a companion, in fact, his "friend and companion" Margo Lane. A woman. Now what exactly was this friend and companion relationship? Today, the tabloids would be all over them.

"I Love a Mystery" had three heroes---Jack, Doc and Reggie---who, as I recall it, spent a lot of time in the Cave of the Bats. This trio have undoubtedly gone on to their just rewards but when I think of them that's where they are, still in the Cave of the Bats.

What was the name of the spooky show which had that great radio sound effect, the squeaking door? The door was opened by our host Raymond and we knew that behind it was something scary. I just remembered: it was The Inner Sanctum.

I don't know if it was on this or some other spooky show but one radio program I still remember is when some scientists got a chicken heart to double its size. This could have been a good thing but the scientists had neglected to find a way to stop or reverse this process so the chicken heart kept doubling, all the while with the sound of its beat getting louder and louder, until it covered the earth, just like spam, junk mail and cell phones.

Then there were the comedy shows. Jack Benny could be funny just by saying, "Hmmmmm." Fred Allen knocked on the doors in Allen's Alley, encountering Mrs. Nussbaum, Socrates Mulligan, Titus Moody and I can't recall what others. Nowadays, I'm sure the PC police wouldn't allow any of these to appear Charlie McCarthy sparred with Edgar Bergen and, over the radio, you couldn't even see Bergen's lips move.

My wife Beverly says I have to mention her favorite Saturday morning show, Let's Pretend. The thing I remember best about this show is the jingle, "Cream of Wheat is so good to eat/You must have it every day/It's good for growing babies/And grownups too to eat/For all the family's breakfasts/You can't beat Cream of Wheat." I've forgotten many things over the past 60 or more years but not this jingle. And I don't even eat Cream of Wheat.

Well, when I was reminded of Fibber McGee all of these other radio memories tumbled out of the closet of my memory. "Hi, ho Silver, away!" "Who knows what evil lurks . . ." The squeaky door. "Mrs. Nussbaum!" I don't think we'll ever forget any of these. And what do we have today? TV reality shows, multiplying at the rate of that chicken heart. Need I say more?

September and October 2003 Observations

The next two "Observations" are on our first visit to Ireland. Our youngest son Christopher had married an Irish girl, Flindie, who worked in the same Silicon Valley computer company, and her brother Dave was getting married in Killarney. We had a fine time in Ireland and the wedding was unusual, taking place outdoors in a ruined abbey on the island of Inisfallen and presided over by a Druid priestess. At any rate, I thought of the minister as a Druid priestess because the bridesmaids were stationed at the four points of the compass and she referred to the wind and the elements. As described in the second "Observations," the elements seemed to be against the wedding as when we went by boat to the island it was pouring down rain. Then, when the bride arrived on the last boat and stepped out onto the island the sun miraculously appeared.

At the time, we weren't aware that Chris and Flindie were considering a move from Silicon Valley to Ireland and that we'd be making annual trips to Ireland to see them and then to see our two grandchildren, Logan and Stephanie. Well, it's a good thing we liked Ireland so much.

Observations Goes to Ireland

Faithful Observations readers may remember that about two years ago I reported on the wedding of our youngest son, Chris, to Florinda (Flindie) McCarthy of Ireland. We were invited to visit Ireland, a place we'd never been, and as Flindie's brother David was getting married there in July this seemed a good time to go. We went on a week's tour first, starting at Bunratty (close to Shannon airport) and ending in Killarney, where our in-laws had just built a new house and where the wedding would take place.

The first observation to make about Ireland is that just about everything you've seen about it in movies or read about it in books is true. The Emerald Island is indeed green. Many residents, as testified by store and pub signs, have Irish names---O'Shea, O'Neill, O'Brien, Quill, Fitzgerald, etc. There are many pubs, over 30 on the main street of one small town we drove through (our tour director told us). As for the weather, we were told the now late Bob Hope had said Ireland is the only country to have all four seasons in one day and this was also true.

There's more to be said about the weather. It rained at some point during every day we were there, which is why Ireland is green (and why I carried my raincoat at all times.) But most days also had their dry, if cloudy, periods and, especially during out stay in Killarney, there were long periods of sunshine (making me feel foolish about carrying my raincoat). So, if like us, you monitor the weather in Ireland and see forecasts of rain or showers for every day don't cancel your trip; it won't be that wet (and in any case it will be delightfully cool as compared to our summer weather).

A word about driving in Ireland. Not only do the Irish drive on the wrong side of the roads but those roads are interesting. If you look down many of the secondary ones, especially those with no lines in the middle, you'll swear they are one way only. But then you'll find that when a car comes along in the opposite direction you can get past without actually hitting it. It seems that someone in Ireland has measured the roads exactly so that two cars, small ones, can just barely pass each other. The saving grace about driving in Ireland is that the motorists, unlike, say, in Italy, are so polite and in the towns cars actually stop for pedestrians instead of trying to hit them (like, say, in Italy).

About Irish cuisine, if you like boiled or mashed potatoes then this is for you as these are served with just about any meal (if you want fried potatoes, ask for chips). You can get a good meal in pubs. I had one of the best fish and chips lunches I've ever had in a pub; the fish was plaice. The Irish breakfast is eggs with sausages and what looks like Canadian bacon plus tomatoes. The Irish seem to be averse to soft eggs so I switched to scrambled and found out that this on toast is not bad. Beverly tried steak and mushroom and shepherd's pie as well as a dish called boxty, a potato crepe with meat filling, and gives them all a thumbs up. As for drink, I happen to like dark beer and when I was told that Guinness was not only dark but healthy (full of iron) this became my daily fare. Incidentally, Irish Guinness is much smoother and creamier than what we get here.

If there's any establishment in Ireland more prevalent than pubs it's the bed and breakfast. These are everywhere and even in the most remote mountain area you look around and there's a B&B. If you're driving through Ireland you'll always be able to find a bed and breakfast and at a much lower price than a hotel.

As for attractions, Ireland is full of ABC's, our tour guide's name for "another bloomin' castle" (or church), century-old stone ruins, interesting shops with relatively inexpensive goods (sweaters, linens, crystal), and of course there's the fabulous scenery. But even more than the scenery what makes visiting Ireland so pleasant is the friendliness of the people. As already noted, the cars stop for pedestrians and this is but one example; the people are just plain nice and will go out of their way to make your stay there an enjoyable one. (I must mention that on our visit to an ABC, Blarney Castle, while in the Blarney Woolen store, I heard a voice say, "Martin, is that you?" and there were Ted Katoff and his wife Mary, newly elected SRC Board member, showing that no matter where you go you can't away from Sun City).

Well, I'd intended to write about the wedding we attended, on Innisfallen, an island with nothing on it but seventh century ruins, but have run out of space, and, come to think of it, the wedding deserves a piece by itself. So tune in to future Observations, and, if you haven't gone to Ireland yet, by all means do so. Erin go braugh!

Observations Goes to Ireland---II

At the end of last month's Observations I said I'd be writing about the wedding we attended during our July visit to Ireland. But my wife Beverly told me I'd been pretty skimpy in describing the attractions we'd been to in case any readers were thinking of a trip to that country. So, first, a few of those attractions.

If you fly into Shannon airport, as we did, nearby Bunratty has a castle and a folk park, a famous pub called Dirty Nellie's and a Blarney Woolen Mills outlet, enough for a day or so visit while you're getting over jet-lag. The castle has medieval dinners and the folk park has a dinner show with Irish singing and dancing. If Dirty Nellie's is too crowded or smoky, you can have a good pub meal (we had an early dinner) at the Creamery.

While we stayed in Bunratty (in the Bunratty Castle hotel) our tour took us to the Cliffs of Moher on the Western coast, where you can see the Atlantic waves crashing on the rocks. Our tour then headed east to Dublin with a stop at the Waterford crystal factory. Dublin has one of those on-and-off bus tours and if we hadn't been in our own tour we'd have taken this. A must stop is Trinity College, which houses the Book of Kells, an illuminated manuscript of the four gospels.

If you want to spend some time in an Irish town you can't do better than Killarney, where we stayed for ten days, first at the Best Western International hotel, where we had two excellent dinners, then at the Oaklawn House B&B just a few minutes from town center, where the gardens, tended daily by Patrick O'Connell, are beautiful and the Irish breakfasts, prepared by his wife Rosemary, are grand, then finally at the home of our daughter-in-law's parents, Ol and Mags, where we received "cead mile failte," a hundred thousand welcomes.

Killarney is a great stopping place not only because of its many shops and eating places but because from there you can take a number of interesting one-day trips. West of Killarney, three peninsulas project out into the Atlantic. The best-known (and middle one) is the Iveragh Peninsula, containing the Ring of Kerry, which was included in our tour. The Dingle (top) and the Beara (bottom) Peninsulas offer equally fine drives, from mountain passes to beaches, with magnificent views one after another. If you're not driving, tours can be arranged from the Irish Tourist Office in downtown Killarney.

Getting back to Killarney itself, from downtown you can walk into the Killarney National Park, which contains Ross Castle. Alternately, you can take a horse-and-buggy into the park and have the driver tell you all about it. Muckross House, a Victorian mansion with beautiful grounds, is a ten-minute drive from downtown and well worth a half-day visit. Torc waterfall is another few minutes down the road. The Tourist Office told us the best restaurant in Killarney was Bricin's and after having a lunch and a dinner there we agreed. Tell owner Johnny MacGuire you're from Sun City in California if you go there.

Okay, finally, the wedding. It was on Innisfallen Island, which has nothing on it except ruins of a seventh century monastery. Considering Ireland's uncertain weather it seemed incredibly optimistic (or foolhardy) to have a wedding there. We learned that this had been done only once before, 20 years ago. When we got into our little outboard motor-driven boats at Ross Castle to go to the island and it began pouring down rain the idea really seemed foolhardy. But, as the groom David later said, when the bride Nicki, in the last boat, set foot on the island, to the accompaniment of bagpipes, miraculously the rain stopped, the sun came out and all was beautiful. Maybe it was the influence of the woman who performed the ceremony, who, we were told, was in tune with the spirits, or the groom's Aunt Moura, a retired nun who'd brought a unity candle, or just the luck of the Irish.

In any case, under a warm sun and in the monastery ruins, the guests formed a ring, the bridesmaids were stationed north, south, east and west, the woman talked of the winds and the elements, bride and groom read their vows, afterwards the bagpiper played, and Hollywood couldn't have written a better script.

There's an epilogue. The reception was in a hotel (on the mainland) and lasted well into the next morning. When Beverly and I took a taxi back to our B&B at around one AM the driver told us that he'd been a guest at that one previous wedding on Innisfallen Island 20 years before and he pointed out the house now lived in by the couple who'd been wed, still together and with a happy family, a good omen for David and Nicki and on this fine note we'll end.

November 2003 Observations

The "Observations" below was on the election of Arnold Schwarzenegger as Governor of California. As I recall, Gray Davis had made a mess of things and Arnold was supposed to straighten things out. We know how that went.

I know that faithful readers would like even more details of our expedition to Ireland but after two Observations on this had decided to move on to an entirely different topic. Then it came to my attention, as it was on television 24/7, that a recall election was going on in California. Here was a once in a life opportunity that I couldn't resist so here are some Observations on our recall.

Like everyone else, I carefully looked over the list of 315 candidates, seeing if anyone on it sounded like a good prospective governor. There was Paul "Chip" Mailander, a golf professional; since golfing is important to us senior citizens, maybe "Chip" was a prospect. Then there was Mike P. McCarthy, a used car dealer. It's been said of a number of politicians that you wouldn't buy a used car from them. And here was someone who actually was a used car dealer. Leo Gallagher, a comedian, wanted to be governor. Well, no matter what else, maybe he could keep us laughing. Then there's Gary Coleman; uh, oh, better not go there as the National Association for the Protection of Short Afro-American Actors would get on me. As for "adult" film star Mary Carey, some guys I know were all for her but she, like Gary, fell a little short. Okay, that's terrible so I'll apologize and, while I'm at it I'll apologize in advance if any of the candidates mentioned happen to read this; just having a little fun is all.

As it turned out, comedian Leo Gallagher got almost 5,000 votes, showing that quite a few people, after the grim Gray Davis years, wanted some comic relief. Mike McCarthy had about 1,200 votes, so, yes, there are some who'll vote for a used car dealer, maybe people who;d gotten good deals from him. Golfer "Chip" Mailander garnered over 600 votes so will have to remain on the links rather than move into the Capitol and frankly being on a golf course sounds better to me. I noticed that Arianna Huffington and Bill Simon both got a considerable number of votes and they weren't even running. I suppose the only thing you can say is that the people who voted for them weren't going to be deterred by anything, or maybe it's just California.

At 8:01 PM on election night the outcome was announced, No on Davis and Yes on Arnold. This didn't stop the TV channels for devoting hours to the election, with the usual "experts" all holding forth. And I'm sure that in the coming days we'll have even more hours of speculation on how Arnold will do as Governor. Since I know about as little as the "experts," I'll so a little speculating of my own. When Arnold first appears before the Legislature will he be carrying one of those big guns he used in his films and then say, "Just kidding, guys." Will Cruz Bustamante be relegated to a broom closet down the hall of the Capitol? Will TV start showing all of Arnold's old movies? Will the media use the word "terminate" millions of times? Will Californians now, instead of saying, "See ya," say "Hasta la vista"?

Well, the people have spoken and, improbable as it may seem, California now has a movie actor as its Governor, certainly a first. Wait a minute, almost forgot about Ronald Reagan. How Arnold does remains to be seen but our state will not lack for media attention So, good luck to Governor Schwarzenegger (spelling that name is a challenge); you've done it in Hollywood and maybe now you can do it in Sacramento. Hasta la vista.

2004 OBSERVATIONS

January 2004 Observations

In the "Observations" below I both looked back at the previous year and looked ahead to the current year, 2004. I see I mentioned three trials, that of Kobe Bryant, Scott Peterson and Michael Jackson. I don't believe that Kobe's case ever went to trial; if it did I can't remember what happened. At any rate, Kobe emerged unscathed and he led the Lakers to the NBA title last year so he's once again a hero. Did anyone mention Tiger Woods? Yes, in time the furor about Tiger's transgressions will abate and if he comes back to win the Master's or the U.S. Open he'll once again be a hero. We know that Michael Jackson is no longer around for the media to shout about. As for Scott Peterson, I wonder how many people remember him. As stated before, there's nothing so out-of-date than last year's big news story and that was about six years ago.

Observations on the Year Behind and the Year Ahead

The year 2003 was a significant one and, no, not only because of Michael Jackson. Our country invaded Iraq, the first time we've waged a pre-emptive war. In California, we recalled our governor in another first. Closer to home, our Sun City Roseville fees took their biggest ever jump and the fiscal woes of our golf course and restaurant made it to the local newspaper.

You don't have to be much of a prophet to see that the year 2004 is going to be an even more significant one than the year we've just left behind. Our invasion of Iraq was an unqualified success but now we're left with the task of rebuilding that country, establishing a democracy while providing security, all in the face of what we're now calling "insurgent" attacks.

In California, the voters have spoken and thrown out the politicians, or at least the governor, who got us into our budgetary mess. The question in 2004 is whether Arnold can get us out, or at least make a start on it. As for Sun City, efforts will be made to turn the golf course and restaurant around; let's hope they succeed. Judging by the success of our neighboring casino, maybe putting some slot machines in the Lodge would do the trick.

Now that these matters are out of the way, let's have some fearless predictions for the coming year. One, the media will relentlessly follow every move of Michael Jackson. In between this coverage, the Scott Peterson trial, if there's anything left after that lengthy pretrial hearing, will be a media circus a la the O.J. Simpson trial. Attorney Mark Gallegos, representing both Scott Peterson and Michael Jackson, will be asking for a continuance for one trial so that he can fly off to the other. Meanwhile, in Colorado, Kobe Bryan, who somehow managed to find a lawyer other than Gallegos, will have his own media circus, if the media can tear itself away from Michael Jackson. CNN might possibly ask that all three trials be combined (a three-ring circus?) to cut down on their costs.

Maybe the Jackson, Kobe and Peterson trials can't be combined for the sake of television (there are still some rules, even in California) but why not combine all those so-called realty shows into one, something like The Bachelor and Bachelorette find the Fear Factor on the Survivor's Island and everyone gets thrown into the ocean. For those few remaining non-realty dramas, we know that in order to entice viewers back the next season there has to be a cliff-hanger in which one or more of the characters dies, or seems to. So in the West Wing, a bomb blows up the White House and we wonder who's left, Josh or Toby or one of those other fast-talking guys. In ER, the hospital blows up and we wonder who's left, if anyone is left who hasn't been killed by a helicopter or gone off to Africa. In Friends, a bomb blows up the apartment and . . . What, you say this is Friends last season anyway? That's all right, let's still blow them all up and make sure.

As for movies, come to think of it, Observations hasn't gone to enough in the past two years to even comment on them. Still. it's safe to say there'll be a lot of movies about comic strip characters, a lot about teenagers and their trials and tribulations and, for the summer, an epic or two. In December, there may even be a few good films for Oscar time. One thing for certain, there won't be another Terminator sequel, at least not in Hollywood. That will take place right here in Sacramento.

Oh, yes, I just remembered something else that's coming up next year, the presidential election. In 2000, Florida challenged California's status as the nation's goofiest state. Can they do it again? With the Michael Jackson and Peterson trials, California will have established a commanding lead, but anything can happen. For the good of everyone, let's hope the election is a landslide one way or another. Whatever comes, happy 2004.

March 2004 Observations---on the Good Old TV Days

I ended my last month's Observations by contrasting the golden age of radio with today's TV reality shows. My wife and I, surfing TV channels during the holiday interlude, when nothing but reruns or reality shows or reruns of reality shows are shown, came across an episode of the old Bill Cosby show and this led me to thinking of the golden days of television.

Today's young TV viewers have probably never heard of Bill Cosby but readers of our generation will remember that his show was one of the most successful ever and watching just this one episode reminded us why. While so-called reality shows are about phony people in contrived situations, the Cosby show was about a real family involved in situations common to all families. In this episode, the Cosbys, or Huxtables, visit the apartment of their recently married, and now pregnant, daughter and her husband, who are determined to "make it on their own." The apartment has rusty water, a broken window, exposed electrical wires, a temperamental stove, a noisy neighbor and a bad landlord.

The Huxtables, not wanting their future grandchild to grow up in this environment, do what we as parents would do, offer to finance a move to a more suitable place. The youngsters at first turn them down but eventually accept. This will also probably seem familiar to many readers. All of the Huxtable family members are likeable; all have their little foibles. Their show was not filled with insults, innuendo, overt sex, obscenity and nudity, the standard fare of most sitcoms today. In other words, television, like radio, used to be a hell (uh, oh, obscenity), a heck of a lot better than it is today.

I can remember other sitcoms of yesteryear that we used to look forward to watching. There was the Mary Tyler Moore show, with spunky Mary trying to make her way in the world; Lou Grant, who "hates" spunk; Rhoda, Mary's down-to-earth friend from New York; and, speaking of characters with foibles, Ted Knight, the vain but impregnable anchorman, and Sue Anne, the happy homemaker. Another classic sitcom was The Odd Couple, in which the pairing of super-neatnik Felix with hyper-sloppy Oscar was a sure guarantee of laughter. Others that come to mind are Cheers, All in the Family and of course that classic, Mash. No, I haven't forgotten Seinfeld, but the reruns are still going strong so I feel it's never gone away.

Going back even further to the early days of television, there was the Show of Shows, still probably the best TV variety show of all time. ("What's a variety show?" the youngsters will ask. Someday we'll have to explain, when we tell them about washboards, ice boxes, cars with running boards and houses that cost only as much as today's cars). Sid Caesar, a certifiable genius (if not lunatic), Imogene Coca, Carl Reiner and Howie Morris, an unbeatable line-up. Then the dramas, with plays written by such talents as Paddy Chayevsky ("Marty") and with actors such as Paul Newman and other future stars.

Well, enough of this. In the light of what passes for television entertainment today, it's too depressing to remember what we had in the past. Yes, there are still some worthwhile programs scattered in between the endless reality shows and other junk. But you have to work hard to find these and, just when you've become interested, there's a hiatus of weeks or a change of schedule or one of your favorites is put up against another of your favorites. If your favorite is really good it is of course cancelled. The worst case I can recall is the cancellation of an hour show set in a college, The Education of Max Bickford, starring Richard Dreyfuss and Laura Linney, two Academy Award winners no less, with an excellent supporting cast and literate scripts which had the actors talking in whole sentences and actually sounding as if they could be college faculty.

I do want to end this piece by mentioning my personal favorite TV hour, 8 to 9 PM Saturday on Channel 6, two English comedies in a rare bit of sensible programming by our public channel. At 8 is As Time Goes By, about an older English man and woman who meet again after having been separated during the Korean War, starring Dame Judi Dench (another Oscar winner). At 8:30 is Waiting for God, about the residents of an English retirement community, some of whom may be similar to residents you know in Sun City. Quick, start watching these shows before Channel 6 moves them to midnight or cancels them.

April 2004 Observations

The "Observations" below was my first on Things Guaranteed to Happen, or TGH's, a close cousin to Life's Little Annoyances, LLA's. I see that, as was the case with LLA's, I didn't refer to TGH's in the first go-around. I noted that in the home, appliances invariably broke down on Fridays or on weekdays, when either there's no service available or, if there is, it costs double or triple what it does on weekdays. That's a typical TGH and is certainly as true today as it ever was. I also noted that if you're expecting an important phone call the next call you get will be from some stranger, usually asking for money. Again, this is still a TGH.

Observations on Things Guaranteed to Happen

Different people hold different views on how the world operates. Some believe that everything is preordained, others that all is random. Some think life follows a divine plan, others that there's no reason to anything. But no matter what our world view, there seem to be a number of things that are built into the fabric of life, that in my experience are guaranteed to happen.

One thing that is certain to happen is this: you make a medical appointment and, as you're in an HMO, it's for a day six months down the road. No matter what, on that particular day something else is sure to come up. The rest of that week, the entire month, is clear, but on that day there'll be a conflict.

Let's say you have re-scheduled your medical appointment and are in your car driving to your HMO, which says you should be there 15 minutes early to sign in. So you're not dawdling. Guaranteed to happen: you'll get behind the world's slowest driver. That driver finally turns off, without signaling, of course. Guaranteed to happen: you'll hit every red light on the way. Finally, you arrive. Guaranteed to happen: someone will dart into the last available parking space. Okay, you've finally parked, found the right office and have signed in (late). Guaranteed to happen? You've guessed it. There's a two hour wait.

Many of the things that are guaranteed to happen occur in the home. First of all, if something breaks down, like the heater in winter or the air-conditioner in summer, it will always be on a weekend, or at best late on Friday afternoon. This will make it almost impossible to get any repair person to come out. If you somehow do, you'll have to pay double, maybe triple, the normal rate.

Other appliances also have the ability to know exactly when to stop working. If you're giving a big dinner party, the stove will suddenly give out. If you've just returned from a trip with a load of dirty clothes, the washer or dryer, or perhaps both, will malfunction. The most likely time for your television set to go blank is just before the Super Bowl.

Other things in the home guaranteed to happen: if you're expecting an important phone call, the next time the phone rings it'll be a sales person or a wrong number. When the call does come, the pen or pencil you've put out to take down the information is no longer there. A few more things: if you place some object on a flat surface, it will somehow manage to slide off. Towels in particular like to do this. If you're settling down to read a good book after a hard retirement day, the light bulb in your lamp will go out and you'll have get up to replace it. If you need a flashlight for any reason, none of the half dozen or so you know you have is where you thought it was.

Travel is another area where certain things are guaranteed to happen. Just before you're about to leave, one of the wheels on your best suitcase will come off. The electrical adaptors you used on your last trip and carefully put away will have disappeared. The passports you know are in your desk are also gone, maybe to the same place.

I almost forgot something and that is the device I'm now writing on. If your computer server makes any kind of change there's guaranteed to be a problem. Your password will suddenly be invalid or your computer will freeze up or maybe your screen will just go blank. If you have something important to send to someone, your e-mail will stop working and . . . Uh, oh, before something happens I'd better get this in to the Sun Senior News. So, see you next month. Before then, lots of other unwanted things will have happened. That's guaranteed.

May 2004 Observations

A reprise of my first "Observations" on Sun City, this one after being there six years. People were getting older so less golfers, less tennis players, less active club members. This trend of course continues to the current day, only even more so. I noted that as you aged retirement didn't get any easier, but concluded that it was still better than working. I'd say the same today.

Observations after Six Years at Sun City Roseville

The first Observations I wrote for the Sun Senior News was about four years ago. It was "Observations after Living in Sun City Roseville for Two Years." One of my observations then was that the parking lot at the Lodge is always filled up with cars but when you go into the Lodge nothing special is going on and there's almost no one in there. So where, I asked, do all the people go?

I've been reminded of this observation because this year I've started to play pool in the mornings and when I arrive at the Lodge I usually have to go to the outer reaches (Rocklin, as one of my fellow pool players says) of the parking lot to find an empty space. But when I go into the Lodge, except for a few pool players and others, there's nobody there. So, in the last four years nothing has changed and the question, "Where do all the people go?" remains unanswered.

Another observation made four years ago was that if you get to a Sun City event on time you'll be lucky to get in as everyone else has gotten there at least half an hour early. I was reminded of this when my wife Beverly and I recently went on a trip to Reno. The flyer said to be at the Lodge to board the bus by 9 AM. To be sure to get there on time, we left about 20 minutes of nine and were at the Lodge by ten of. Needless to say, we were the last persons there. I've speculated before on the compulsion of us older folk to be overly punctual. Maybe it's because experience has taught us to be wary of life's many perils. The clock may be slow, the car may break down, there might not be room to get into the Lodge parking lot (because of reasons unknown) and, as in life in general, we want to make sure we don't miss the bus.

But there have been changes here during the past four years. One obvious observation is that people in Sun City have gotten older. This is reflected, as everyone knows, in the decline of residents using our golf courses. I play tennis (still), not golf, and here too I've noticed that a number of people I used to play with are no longer seen at the courts. Shoulders, knees and hips seem to be the main culprits in forcing them to the sidelines. In fact, a number of former tennis players I know have, like myself, taken up pool, which is a lot easier on the hips, shoulders and knees.

Another change I've observed is that the number of residents who used to be active in Sun City affairs have, like the number of golfers, decreased in the last few years. I know that the committee I'm on has been seeking some new members, so far in vain, and I've heard that some clubs have had a hard time finding people to be officers. I guess this too is to be expected as Sun City ages.

Where is this leading? I suppose it's to the observation that retirement isn't all that easy and it doesn't get any easier as we all get older. Still, it's better to be active than not and I'm sure there are Sun City residents who'll step up to fill committee and club positions. And if tennis and even golf, where you don't have to run, have become too strenuous there are other activities like shooting pool, table tennis, bocce and bowling that are available to us. Finally, when I meet younger people who are still working and hear about all their problems---the commute, office politics, cutbacks and downsizing—I have to observe that, all in all, I'd just as soon be retired.

June 2004 Observations

With the "Observations" below on our denigrating society I joined the many writers who lamented the decline of civility in our country and the partisanship in our politics. As I recall, current President Obama's initial campaign promise, which had great appeal, was to end the partisanship in Washington. Guess this didn't happen. If anything, things have gotten even worse. Well, there's always hope, but as of now this "Observations" remains one of my most pertinent ones.

Observations on our Denigrating Society

As this is being written, it's that time of the year again, the NBA playoffs, which are not quite as long as the regular season, it only seems that way. I of course will be rooting for the Kings once again. I don't know if this will be their year but one thing I do know, if they don't make it they'll be denigrated as the worst of bums.

So far this season, the Kings have been great; then, after Chris Webber returned and they had a spate of injuries, they were terrible; after they beat the Mavs in the first round of the playoffs they were good, if not exactly great, once again. If they win the championship they'll definitely be great; in fact, the greatest. Coach Rick Adelman will be a genius. Even Webber will be hailed for his comeback from injury. But if the Kings falter along the way the players will have failed in the clutch and trades will be demanded. Coach Adelman will be denounced as a first-class dunce. In sports nowadays, you're either a champion or a chump. There doesn't seem to be any in-between.

The worst case of sports denigration annually occurs with the Super Bowl. Only one team can win it and thus become the football champion for that year. The losing team will be relegated to the role of also-rans. It won't matter that to reach the Super Bowl they must have been pretty good. As for the rest of the teams, it won't matter if a few of them won division championships and if some others had decent seasons. They'll all be consigned to the ash heap, all losers for that year.

Somewhat akin to this type of sports denigration is the demonization that's become so common in our political discourse. Does anyone remember Bill Simon? Probably not. He was the businessman who ran for governor against Gray Davis in 2002. He was portrayed as a crook, a swindler, a cheat. Davis may not have been good at being Governor but he and his forces were very good as demonizing their opponents. I remember thinking that after the election Bill Simon, if he was half as bad as portrayed, is certainly going to end up going to jail. So what happened? The election ended, we stopped hearing what a terrible guy Simon was and, if I recall correctly, he even made a try at running in the recall.

The current presidential campaign has already demonized both candidates; well, President Bush and "presumptive candidate" John Kerry (and wasn't there a time that the campaigns, and the mud-slinging, didn't start until after Labor Day?) Bush is said to be a liar, a bungler and a complete idiot. Kerry is a waffler who's withheld, or voted to withhold, vital equipment from our military. I'll venture a guess that after the election both men will return to being guys with virtues and faults who've done good things and made some mistakes; in other words, just human beings like the rest of us. As for the campaign issues---Iraq, the economy, gay marriages or whatever, only history will decide, and maybe not even then. After all, we're still re-fighting Vietnam.

Going back to the immediate concern, here's wishing luck to the Kings. No matter what happens in the next playoff round, and in the round after that and after that and after that, if they get that far, they've once again had a good season, provided a lot of entertainment and excitement for their fans, and have done their best despite injuries and distractions. Even if this turns out not to be their year (again), I hope they'll all be back for another try next season. And they won't be bums.

Aug 2004 Observations---Goes Cruising (Yet Again)

Faithful Observations readers (thousands: okay, dozens, of you) know that my wife Beverly and myself are addicted to cruising. This summer, in order to get away from the usual valley heat, we thought it would be a good idea to take a week's cruise to Alaska. As it turned out, that week marked the peak of a heat wave in Alaska. As one of our fellow passengers remarked, our Alaskan cruise felt more like a Caribbean one. Luckily, among the coats, jackets, hats and scarves we'd packed, we'd thrown in a few lightweight clothes.

We'd booked this cruise early in the year, on by far the largest ship we'd ever been on, a brand-new one holding almost 3,000 passengers. If you included the crew, there were about as many people on board as living her in Sun City. Even with the map provided, it wasn't easy to find our way around and it wasn't unusual to encounter passengers wandering around in the halls, asking: Where's our dining room? Where's the so-and-so lounge? Where's our room? Where are we? At least we were on a ship and so couldn't get completely lost. As with a Las Vegas casino, it wasn't until the end of the week that we had things pretty well figured out, and by then the voyage was over. Oh, well, if we ever take this ship again . . .

One of the things we noticed on this cruise was the large number of families on board, and by families I mean sons and daughters, grandsons and granddaughters, maybe even nieces and nephews, large groups. The ship seemed to be prepared for this, with special areas designated as "kid" zones and more "kid" activities than even at a summer camp. It led me to wonder if this is becoming a trend, and if, along with their cell phones, computers and DVD's, the new generation will be expecting as a matter of course to go on cruises.

Nutritionists are concerned about obesity among the young. If more and more children are taken on cruises, this will become an even greater concern. As we all know, one of the big things about cruising, maybe the biggest, is eating. A cartoon in the latest New Yorker shows a cruise ship with the name S.S. All You Can Eat. Huge as it was, the ship had five different dining rooms plus two buffets that could have been named CNN as they were open 24/7.

The ship's paper noted that the food supplies used each week included 5,056 pounds of steak, 8, 428 pounds of potatoes, 1,673 pounds of pasta, 2,718 pounds of French fries, 1,278 pounds of lobster tail and 42,000 pounds of breakfast pastries. They also included 37, 203 pounds of fresh vegetables and 38,709 pounds of fresh fruit, so at least we can say we were eating a lot of healthy stuff as well as all those desserts.

Despite the unusually warm weather, Alaska, with its natural beauty, colorful past and always friendly people, was again a fascinating place to visit. It was amazing to be reminded of the lengths that people were willing to go in hopes of striking it rich by finding gold, climbing up steep snowy mountains with thousands of pounds of gear, then building boats to cross rivers, and only then arriving at a gold rush camp with thousands of others and no guarantee of finding anything. It seems the smart ones were those who didn't try to find gold but provided something the gold miners wanted, like fresh fruit, or available women. Aside from visiting ashore, it was nice on board ship for us valley dwellers to look at a large body of peaceful water and the glaciers behind it.

Well, we're home again. We can't expect our cabin boy Albert to put our bedroom and bathrooms in apple-pie order as he did every day on the cruise. We can't debate about which dining room to choose for that night or which show to see. Next time I expect we'll look for a somewhat smaller ship, but Observations will keep on cruising.

September 2004 Observations

I see from the "Observations" below that we got our two cats about 5 ½ years ago. They're the first male cats we've had and they've grown to a considerable size. Shandyman is still Shandyman but Cinderbun's name has become simply "Bun-Bun."

To our regret, neither has become a real lap cat like some (females) we've had before. Bun-Bun curls up every night on the footrest of Beverly's chair but won't sit in her lap. Maybe he has a foot fetish. Shandyman will sit in my lap or. more accurately, on my chest with his nose an inch from mine, but he's too restless to stay there for very long and after a while he'll jump off and look for some other form of entertainment. There are times when the cats are exasperating, but, as long-term "cat people" we're glad we got them from the Placer SPCA. Plus, our two grandchildren who live in Rocklin like them and come over probably more to chase the cats than to visit us.

Observations Looks at Kittens

On Tuesday, July 6, my wife Beverly and I went to the Placer SPCA and adopted two stray kittens, both male. One was black with a white patch on his chest. His SPCA name was Cinder. The other was black and white. His SPCA name was Andre. Our beloved cat Mickey had passed away shortly after Thanksgiving last year. We'd had our grieving period and thought it was time to fill the void that Mickey had left.

When you get two kittens, you know that they'll spend a lot of time scuffling. Cinder was already neutered so we were able to bring him home from the SPCA with us. Andre had to go to the vet's to be neutered so we didn't get him home until that Friday. As soon as we introduced him to Cinder they sprang at each other, grappled and rolled around on the floor. We watched them apprehensively, afraid they might be fighting to the death but they emerged from their scuffle unharmed. We went to bed that first night hoping for the best. When we opened our bedroom door the next morning we found them sleeping together on top of their scratching post. So they were compatible. A big sigh of relief.

We couldn't just accept the SPCA names, so in a week or so Cinder became Cinderbun. Beverly looked up baby names and found out Shandy meant mischievous boy so Andre became Shandyman (or Shandybun or Shandydandy). The two kittens soon displayed different personalities. Cinder is quicker, jumps higher, loves people, snuggles into laps and purrs like a jet plane. Shandy is more persistent when he wants something (like your lunch) and loves to bathe, mostly Cinder, but anyone else if he gets the chance, also purrs loudly and sits on laps but doesn't snuggle in as much.

Both kittens are insatiably curious and both can move at the speed of light. You see one of them sitting on a chair in the breakfast nook, go to open the bedroom door and in an instant a kitten has darted in. You check around carefully, no kittens in sight, open a closet door and two kittens are in there, exploring your clothes. You open the refrigerator door and two kittens are sniffing to see what's stored in there. Beverly has to be careful whenever she opens the dishwasher or else she might be washing a kitten as well. They like to get under our bed and then, if you walk by, you'll feel a paw on your foot. They can also get into any space, as behind our television set. They're also both very interested in the television, watching the picture and putting their paws on the screen.

And they are both very interested in my computer. In fact, Cinderbun right now keeps jumping up on my keyboard, causing me to retype this as he keeps hitting the number 3. And yesterday, when Shandyman was watching me type, he kept trying to get the curser as it moved across the screen.

We had quite a few kitten toys on hand but the things they most like to play with are a long cord, plastic milk container tops, any other kind of bottle cap, any kind of string, including shoe laces, paper bags and a little woolen ball. It's a good thing they like that piece of cord because when, as kittens do, they suddenly disappear, they can be lured from their hiding place, usually under the bed, by dragging the cord along the floor.

Above all, Cinder and Shandy are incredibly cute. When they finally exhaust themselves and cuddle up on our laps, whatever mischief they've gotten into is forgiven. We find that during the day we keep asking one another, "Where are they?" and "What are they doing?" Our house is no longer empty but is full of life, two kitten lives.

October 2004 Observations

At the time of the "Observations" below I was headed to my 75th birthday and it occurred to me that I'd been around for a long time. Members of the previous generation had seen tremendous changes in their lifetimes: the assembly line, the auto, the airplane, the telephone, the radio, television, the washing machine, the refrigerator, and so on and on. The changes in my lifetime had been almost as great, even greater in some respects. The computer had transformed the way we communicate, do business, live. Television had taken over a large part of our lives. Air travel has developed to a point where we can travel anywhere. Medicine has prolonged our lives. In the last few years, there've been even more changes. I see that I was a prophet in predicting that cell phones would eventually have all kinds of attachments, such as digital cameras and TV's, like a Swiss army knife. I didn't foresee the "smart" phones with millions of applications that will do almost anything. I said that my grandson will be living in an entirely different world from ours. At the rate we're going, we may be living in an entirely different world in a few years.

Observations on Changes During Last 75 Years

In a couple of months I will amazingly have been on this planet for 75 years, three-quarters of a century. This has led me to think about the changes that have occurred in my lifetime. Just looking around our house, there is, for example, the telephone. I don't know how old I was when my parents first got a telephone but I remember that it rarely rang as almost everyone we knew lived on the same street and it was easier to just yell out the window. If the phone did ring, it was a tense moment as it probably meant bad news. Now, everyone has a cell phone and people call each other all the time. "I'm in the car. I'm getting out of the car. I'm going into the supermarket. I'm in the produce section. I'm buying oranges." And so on.

When I was a kid we used to rush home on Sunday nights to listen to the radio. The Shadow ("Who knows what evil lurks in the hearts of men?"), Jack Benny, Charlie McCarthy, Fred Allen. During the week it was Jack Armstrong, the All-American Boy, Henry Alrdich, the Great Gildersleeve, the Lone Ranger and of course the Inner Sanctum. When I returned from the Army in 1954 we didn't yet have a television set but some of my parents' friends had so I could go over and watch basketball on a tiny black-and-white screen instead of listening to it on the radio. Then came color, then bigger and bigger sets, then digital and now TVs the size of movie screens.

I remember when the iceman used to come around and deliver chunks of ice, which he carried in a pair of tongs, for our ice box. I also used to watch the coal trucks come and deliver their coal down a chute into the basement of our apartment building. The coal somehow provided steam heat during the winter. I don't know when our family replaced the ice box with a refrigerator but that was the end of the ice man.

In the summer the thing to do was go to the movies, which were air-conditioned, and so escape from the heat and humidity for a few hours. Going to the movies meant seeing a double-feature, plus the Fox Pathe newsreel and maybe a couple of cartoons (and no commercials). Today we simply click on the thermostat and the air conditioner comes on. Without air-conditioning, what would our Sun Cities be like? Would there even be Sun Cities?

When I went to high school the cool thing was to have a slide rule. Now everyone has those little calculators and the slide rule has gone the way of the ice box. When I graduated from high school I (and most of my friends) were presented with that standard graduation gift, a fountain pen. I believe these are not extinct yet but I haven't owned one for years.

In college, I soon discovered I had to have a typewriter. Anyone remember those? Now kids going to college are provided with computers as a matter of course. I think I still have an old typewriter in the back of one of our closets. I recall spending a lot of time looking up things in the college library. I imagine that today's students simply go the Google on their computers. I also wrote letters home to my parents. Today it's e-mails or cell phone calls.

On August 19 of this year, our first grandson, Mason Lee Green, was born to our son Michael and his wife Bridget. I wonder what changes will occur in Mason's lifetime. Computers the size of credit cards (or do they already have these)? Clothes with built-in air-conditioning so that you remain cool wherever you are? Cell phones with all kinds of attachments---digital cameras, TV's, DVD's, Tebo's, mini-microwaves---like a Swiss army knife. The only sure thing is that Mason's will be an entirely different world with changes we can't begin to imagine. And, yes, I did want to somehow work the announcement of our grandson into these Observations.

2005 OBSERVATIONS

January 2005 Observations

Another "Observations" on the year past, 2004. I see I mentioned Condaliza Rice; wonder what she's doing now. We know that John Kerry is still a Senator. What's happened to John Edwards? (Note: I wrote this before Edwards was outed by the Inquirer. We now know what he was up to). And Chris Weber and Bobby Jackson of the Kings are long gone. Time does fly by.

Observations on the Year Past

The worst thing about 2004's election is that it went on and on and on. The best thing is that this time it mercifully ended on Election Day. .

If the campaign charges of the two parties were to be believed, the nation had a choice between a puffed-up war hero who couldn't make up his mind about anything and a possible National Guard malingerer who'd never admit to making a mistake. A visitor from outer space may well have wondered: how did these two guys ever get nominated as the best our two parties could offer.

As always, stories that seemed so important, at least to the media, while the election was going on and on, disappeared once it was over: Nobody now, not even Dan Rather, seems interested in Bush's National Guard Service (or lack of it), and similarly nobody now (what happened to those swift boat vets) cares about Kerry's Vietnam experience. And what about those other critical stories: what did Bush do before and after the 9/11 attack? what did Kerry do? what about the Cheneys' (whisper) lesbian daughter? what happened to all of those munitions that disappeared in Iraq? I haven't even seen any stories about weapons of mass destruction recently.

One good thing about the daily bombardment of stories (24/7 is the boast) by the media is that each story, involved with the election or not, is almost immediately displaced by the next new, or "hot," item. Who now remembers what the Condaliza Rice crisis was about? What about all those books that came out every other week by disaffected officials attacking the administration? Or the books by his fellow Viet vets attacking Kerry? Even Fahrenheit 411 now seems something from the distant past.

So, what lessons did the election teach us, besides not to watch cable news from March to November? For one thing, that it's possible to win a presidential election without being a skilled debater. For another, that you can't win an election by going out and shooting a goose. Not only didn't Kerry win the NRA vote, he probably lost the goose vote (cooked his own goose, you might say).

To turn now to something really important, once again injuries struck our Sacramento Kings at just the worst time, during the playoffs. Bobby Jackson went down and Chris Weber was still not recovered from his knee surgery. Even so, the Kings almost made it to their conference finals. Depressing news at year's end about another sport, baseball. Some of our biggest baseball sluggers have taken steroids and many statistics, the bedrock of baseball, will be cast in doubt. In the entertainment world, more depressing happenings: so-called reality shows all over TV, rap music, rock music, drugs, shootings, Michael and Janet Jackson and, finally, Donald Trump.

Well, I can't end on such a depressing note, so let's mention a few good things that occurred in 2004: an election in Afghanistan; an election that the people refused to let be hijacked in the Ukraine; a glimmer of hope (now that Arafat is gone) for the Mideast. And, returning to the sports world, an Eastern Conference team that actually played defense defeated the Lakers for the NBA championship. Even better, the Boston Red Sox, trailing the Yankees three games to zero, won the American League pennant and then went on to win the World Series. The Red Sox won the World Series? Truly a miracle, which tells us that anything is possible. The new year is traditionally a time to wipe out the bad things of the past and look forward to the future. So here's to a great year 2005 for everyone.

Feb 2005 Observations---Welcomes Back Jack

Way back last July I wrote an Observations on the past TV season, which turned out to be mostly about the improbable but somehow fascinating spy series "24" and its hero Jack Bauer. As sometimes happens, so much was going on in Sun City at that time that this Observations never was printed. Just today, January 7, the Bee television columnist Rick Kushman had a piece on the start of "24"'s fourth season, which struck my interest as it expressed much the same views about "24" as I had last July so I'm reprising much of that piece and if Rick won't accuse me of plagiarism I won't accuse him, and I did get there first.

My first observation on the past TV season was that nudity and obscenity were all over the place, and this was before Janet Jackson and the election. About "24," I observed that instead of nudity and obscenity, it has a cast of characters and plot twists so ridiculous that you just have to watch it. Needless to say, it's set in Los Angeles. "24," for those who tune into only PBS, is a series with Keifer Sutherland as agent Jack Bauer, which allegedly takes place in a period of 24 hours, and which has ended its third season and threatens, or promises, to return for a fourth. (It has.).

Part of the fun of watching "24" is to see whether Jack, or anyone else, ever eats, sleeps or goes to the bathroom during the 24 hours. As I recall, in the first year's series, Jack did nod off briefly at one time. Since then, he's remained wide awake. Neither has he eaten or gone to the bathroom.

It's also fun to see how the 24-hour concept breaks down. All of the action, and there's a lot of it, is crammed into 24 hours, and during that time Jack and other agents break a Mexican gangster out of jail, fly him down to Mexico, have several hours worth of adventures there, then return to Los Angeles, drive all over that city (and you know how bad the traffic is there) and all of this is supposed to have happened in one day.

The plots of "24," although having more twists and turns than Highway 1, are basically simple. In each series, Jack has to single-handedly prevent some disaster. In the first year, it was the attempted assassination of Parker, a presidential candidate. In the second, it was destruction of Los Angeles by a nuclear bomb. In the third and most recent, it was the unleashing of a deadly virus, first in Los Angeles and then in other cities. Some Northern California viewers (and Kings fans) might think that destroying Los Angeles isn't that bad an idea. And, considering what a mess Parker makes of his presidency, maybe his assassination wouldn't have been so bad, either. Nevertheless, Jack, being the executive producer as well as the star of "24," comes through each time.

Jack is an agent in a governmental agency called CTU, for, I think, Counter Terrorism Unit, although a better name would be Center for the Terminally Unfit, as CTU makes our even our real CIA and FBI look reasonably competent. CTU routinely bungles every one of its operations. They track a bad guy, break into his headquarters guns out, then find he's not there. They actually capture someone, then allow their prisoner to escape. One of their key operatives, after finding out she hasn't caught the deadly virus, is promptly kidnapped by the bad guys. Even their headquarters isn't secure, as it's attacked by bad guy helicopters and a number of minor cast members are mowed down.

Considering its personnel, it's not surprising that CTU is so ineffective. Jack's daughter Kimi, who's 15 in the first series, is now, and she can't be more than 19, another key CTU operative, doing vague things on a computer. Kimi, by going out at night when she wasn't supposed to, in the first series gets kidnapped by the bad guys and nearly allows the assassination attempt to succeed. In the past series, Kimi, sure enough, gets kidnapped again but only briefly. Another key operative, Nina, who's also at one time Jack's mistress, turns out to be a bad person, cold-bloodedly shooting Jack's wife and anyone else in her path and then still trying to seduce poor Jack. Jack eventually captures Nina, but, true to CTU form, she escapes. In the end, Nina almost kills Kimi, who can't bring herself to fire a gun at Nina, but Jack steps in and shoots Nina. It looks as if she's dead but Nina is so truly evil that I can't help but believe the writers will find a way to bring her back next season.

While Jack is pursuing the evildoers, there's always a subplot involving President Parker. In this last series, one of Parker's rich backers threatens to pull out as Parker's brother (and chief, maybe only, advisor) is having an affair with his, the rich backer's, wife. So Parker calls on his ex-wife Sheri, to assist him, which she does by not letting the rich backer's wife give him his medication when he suffers a heart attack (and you thought Clinton and Bush were bad). Not only this, but the President's Los Angeles office seems to be in a deserted warehouse and has windows so it's not even private.

Well, after all this, in the last hour all of course turns out well. Although the bad guys have captured the CTU lady, who's the wife of the CTU head, Jack captures the head bad guy's daughter and when he threatens to expose the daughter to the deadly virus the bad guy caves in and tells all (Nina never would have done this) and the country is saved. This is not before the bad guy with the Los Angeles virus eludes capture in a subway, another CTU bungle (and, yes, Los Angeles has a subway) but this is only so there can be a climatic car chase at the end.

Okay, you get the idea as to how inane, unbelievable and downright ridiculous "24" is. I can't wait until next season's series. What peril will Jack be called upon to defeat? Will Kimi be kidnapped again? And is Nina really dead or will she, or maybe her even more evil twin sister, come back? And how much more nudity and obscenity can TV pile on? My guess is: a lot. As for "24," Kushman tells us that "terrorists are again operating on U.S. soil. Once again, Jack is forced to solve the problem because no one will take his advice. And, once again, "24" is a roller-coaster thrill ride." Jack, welcome back.

April 2005 Observations

The next two "Observations" return to life's little annoyances and note that these seem to arise from devices like computers and cell phones that are supposed to make our lives easier. Both "Observations" express my hatred of automated phone systems, something which has not abated one bit.

Observations on More LLAs

I haven't done an Observations on LLAs (Life's Little Annoyances) for a while, but that doesn't mean they've gone away. In fact, there's more of them around than ever. Let's start with credit cards. These are a perpetual annoyance because no matter what credit card you have the companies that issue them want you to move up to one that sounds better (gold instead of silver, platinum instead of gold) and of course costs more.

But the annoyance doesn't stop there. I recently received a credit card statement with a rather large charge on it. The amount looked familiar. Hadn't I paid that the month before? Well, first I had to locate the previous statement. Annoying. Yes, same charge. Then I had to locate my cancelled checks to see if it was actually paid. Annoying. Yes, it had. Then I had to call the credit card company. Yes, my payment had been received but not until after the next month's statement had been sent. That's what they said anyway. Very annoying.

Okay, that was settled. But then came my computer server. I tried to get on the Internet and, lo and behold, kept getting an error message: username and/or password invalid. Wait a minute, I've used the same name and password for years. What had happened. A call to tech support. The tech had me reset the name and password. I tried again. Same error message. Another call. This time I was asked what phone number the computer was dialing. How should I know. The techie unearthed the number; which the server had discontinued, without bothering to let me know. So it wasn't invalid name and/or password; it was the phone number. I was given a new number to type in. Then I had to call the phone company to make sure it was a local number. An all-around annoying experience.

But that was nothing compared to our experience with the cable company. It started with a seemingly innocuous letter saying that we had to get a digital converter box if we wanted to keep getting HBO. We considered. The Sopranos. Maybe some movies. Okay, we made an appointment to get the box, from 2 to 5. Annoying. The guy came, looked at our living room TV, which was connected to a VCR and a Tivo, said he'd never dealt with a Tivo before. We decided not to let him mess with it, in retrospect a very wise decision.

But we conferred and decided, let them do our bedroom TV, no Tivo, only a VCR. Another appointment, annoying. The guy came, hooked up the box, putting the VCR on top of it. We asked, wasn't that bad for the box? Is that the way he usually did it? He said he did whatever space allowed. Oh. And, oh, yes, the VCR now didn't work. We needed a certain cable. We could get it at Radio Shack. He wrote it down.

When he left we had a chance to look at the instruction book he'd left. The box should have 4 inches of air space above it, not a VCR. Next day I called Radio Shack. No, that wasn't the right cable; that guy didn't know what he was talking about. I won't go into further gory details. Suffice it to say we had the digital converter box removed (yes, still another appointment) and will do without The Sopranos. An annoying experience, to put it mildly.

One final universal annoyance. All the above experiences required calling the company. And you know what that means. Yes, running the gauntlet of the automated phone system. I'd say the worst was the computer server's as you had to listen to their admonishments---are you sure you typed everything in correctly, are you sure all of your connections are tight---before they'd finally allow you to speak to a human being, well, not really a human being, a techie.

As I consider all of these LLAs, it occurrs to me that what they also --credit cards, computers, cable TV -- have in common is that they're supposed to make our lives easier and more enjoyable. Instead, they make our lives more stressful, and, boy, can they be annoying.

May 2005 Observations

I concluded last month's Observations by observing that modern developments such as credit cards, computers and automated phone systems, designed to make our lives easier, had the unintended consequence of making our lives more stressful, not to mention leading to countless annoyances. I can't remember when I started using credit cards but I'm sure they were a great convenience. I no longer had to carry around cash or a check book; all I had to do was whip out my trusty card to pay for things. What could be better?.

Then along came the downside of credit cards: solicitations to get other credit cards every day in the mail, solicitations from my credit card company to upgrade my present card, forgetting to get my payment in on time and being hit by late charges. Then of course there are the really bad consequences: people getting into debt (those cards are so easy to use you can forget that eventually you have to pay up, and at outrageous rates of interest) and in the past few years that most dreaded feature of modern-day life, identity theft. It's enough to make you want to cut up your credit cards and go back to carrying cash and/or a checkbook.

By now almost everyone in Sun City must have a computer. What did we do before we had them? Club news is dispensed by computer. E-mails are used instead of phone calls or letters. Letters? Does anyone actually write these any more? People bank online, pay their taxes online, shop online, have sex (well, no, editor, cut that), anyway, do lots of other stuff online. All well and good. But what happens when the computer goes down? Right; you can't do a thing; you are left high and dry. And as with credit cards, you must be careful of identity theft online, not to mention many other computer scams. Thyen there are those viruses which are everywhere and threaten computer users on a daily basis. I don't think a day goes by when I don't meet someone who has some computer problem or other.

Another modern contrivance that was designed to make life easier and has left a lot of undesirable effects in its wake is the cell phone. A lightweight phone you can take anywhere with you. Freedom from wires. What could be better? I'm sure cell phones often are useful, when your car breaks down, when you're late for an appointment, when something comes up and you have to call. But on the other side there's the sound of a cell phone call when in a restaurant, at the movies, at a concert, at the library, or just walking down the street. And there are the people who use their cell phones to give a blow-by-blow account of their activities (who are the people on the other end of the line, I wonder): I'm in the canned soup section, I'm getting a can of vegetable soup, Campbell's, I've moved over to the cereal aisle, I'm getting a box of Cheerio's, I'm . . and on and on and on. Finally, there are the countless ads and commercials by the cell phone vendors trying to get you to switch to their service. Can you hear me now? Yes, over and over again.

Finally, as last month, I have to conclude with my pet hate, the automated phone system. The companies and other organizations that have installed them (and which one hasn't) will probably argue that these systems make it easier for callers by narrowing down their options (as well as by cutting the company's costs). The problem is that more often than not the reason you're calling doesn't fit into any of the system's options. For example, I recently called an airline because we'd made reservations months ago and in looking through our trip stuff I couldn't find any tickets. I went round and round as the airline wanted me to use the automated system and not talk to an actual person. When I finally reached an actual person (the last one left?) I found out the airline doesn't issue tickets any more. That explained that. Yet another advance; now you don't have to worry about having tickets when you go to the airport. But what if the airline's computer is down? Okay, let's not get into the subject of modern day air travel. I guess we'll survive all these modern enhancements to our lives, even if they drive us up the wall while they're helping us.

June 2005 Observations--- on Life's Little Joys

The last two Observations described some of life's little annoyances (LLA's). A while ago, at the urging of my wife Beverly, I did an Observations on life's little joys (LLJ's), to kind of balance things out (you can tell who's the positive and who's the negative one in our house) and in the interest of domestic harmony I thought I'd try another one of those.

Life's little joys, or at least some things we can be thankful for. Hmm, let me think. Okay, Dennis Rodman isn't playing basketball any more and seems to have dropped out of sight. That's something to be thankful for. Basketball brings to mind the recent ousting of the Kings in the first round of the playoffs. Definitely not an LLJ. But at least Bill Walton wasn't broadcasting the games. Another thing to be thankful for. Let's see, John McEnroe is no longer playing tennis. That's good. He hasn't yet dropped out of sight but his TV talk show, or whatever it was, is no longer on. That's very good. . I'm also thankful that Donald Trump has been fired and his show is off the air. What, it's not? Well, we can always hope.

Speaking of Donald Trump, TV: is in pretty bad shape but it's not all reality shows, not yet. Something to be thankful for. Wait a minute. I just realized that all of these LLJ's are negative ones, things we can be thankful for because they're not happening. Let's try to find some positive LLJ's. There must be some out there. TV is bad, but in fact, a few fairly decent shows have recently popped up. "Lost" is a mishmash and it's hard to imagine a more hapless group of people stranded on an island (they'd all, with the possible exception of Locke, be toast on "Survivors), but it's still intriguing and, who knows, maybe they'll get killed off one by one until the series has to be over.

"Desperate Housewives" is, let's face it, pretty trashy, but it's entertaining trash and doesn't take itself too seriously. And it has some truly vicious characters. "Medium" is another show that departs from the formula of psychic sees crime, solves crime; she does, but it goes down some quirky bypaths. I also like "Jack and Bobby," the series about two brothers, one of whom grows up to be president. The intrusion of presidential matters in the future is the worse thing about this show. The best is the character of the boys' mother, created by Christine Lahti; yes, she can really act.

Back to sports, we have the Kings. Yes, they had a tough season, but to look at the positive side they did win 50 games, again. That's not bad. And they did make the playoffs, again. Remember, there was a time that this would be cause for celebration. As for the future, the Kings have Bibby, Brad Miller and Peja, plus Bobby Jackson. That's not a bad start for a team. (*Note: In 2010 all of these players are gone and some would say so are the Kings. But they do have Tyreke Evans.*) As a New Yorker, I'm a long-time Knicks fan and I wish they were in as good a shape. And remember, the hated Lakers didn't even make the playoffs.

Closer to home, I can think of some things to be thankful for about living in Sun City. When we first moved here, we had to negotiate muddy streets and work machines; it was often dusty and noisy. Now it's an attractive-looking place, with trees getting bigger, front yards nicely laid out, nature areas, enough wildlife to make it interesting when taking a walk. Then there are the many talented Sun City residents---singers, dancers, artists, writers, performers; the many volunteers; the many people who give their time to keep the clubs and other organizations going. All positive things to be thankful for.

Finally, to end on a personal note, I'm thankful that, despite all the travails of air travel, we have the means of getting to see our son and our daughter-in-law who live 6,000 miles away in Ireland, something we'll be doing this month. That's definitely an LLJ.

August 2005 Observations

Another "Observations" on another trip to Ireland, this time after a stop in New York and then a cruise from Nice to Paris. I see that I observed there's no really good way of getting from here to Europe, no matter how you go. The same is true in coming back. I see our return trip took about 27 hours and four separate flights. Maybe taking Valium or something like it to numb you is the answer. I see that I described our adventures at De Gaulle airport, but that I didn't get to our even more harrowing adventures getting from Paris to Ireland, possibly because I intended to write about this separately, or possibly because I didn't want to re-live this experience at that time.

Our son in Ireland had suggested we fly from Paris to Shannon airport by Ryan, Ireland's really cheap airline. First, we had to get from our Paris hotel to a place where we'd get a bus that would take us to a little airport about 45 minutes outside Paris. We had one stroke of luck. I'd anticipated taking a cab to the bus place and trying to give directions to a non-English speaking French cab driver. As we know, the French, alone of all Europeans, don't speak English, or, if they do, they pretend not to. At any rate, our tour guide offered to take us to the James Joyce pub, the bus place. The pub of course was closed. Somehow he found out where the bus place was, a big parking lot with many buses. Then somehow he found out which bus we had to take. There were no signs on the buses and all the French bus drivers were off somewhere taking their cigarette break. Amazingly, we did get to the airport and then the fun began again.

The airport was small, hot and crowded and, unlike any other airport I've ever been in, had no boards showing arriving and departing flights. First, we found out we had to pay a fee for our bags. We did this. Then we found out what terminal we had to be in. The terminal was a mob scene. Two planes were leaving for Ireland, one to Shannon and one to Dublin. Nobody seemed to know which was which. Eventually, we got behind some people who sounded like our Irish in-laws and miraculously finally boarded the right plane, tired, sweaty and resolving never to go to this airport again, maybe never to France again.

Observations on Travel

We've been back a week from a month-long trip, first a quick stop in Long Island, New York, (Longisland with a hard "g" to us New Yorkers), then a cruise in France, then a visit to our son and his wife in Ireland. My first observation is that the older you get the longer it takes to recover from jet lag, especially as our return trip involved four separate airplanes and three airports, not including Sacramento, over a period of some 27 hours. No wonder it seemed like such a long day.

My second observation is that there's no really good way to get from Roseville, or Sacramento, to Europe. Our stop in Long Island, to visit my sister, was meant in part to ease the ordeal of the 6,000 miles journey to Europe. So we were dead-tired our first day at my sister's, the result of arising at three AM to get the airport shuttle at 4:40 so we'd be at the airport two hours ahead of our 6:48 flight. When we arrived at our French destination, JFK to Paris, then a connecting flight to Nice, we were perhaps a little less exhausted than if we'd come from Sacramento but, having flow overnight and not getting to Nice until noon, we were still not exactly raring to go, except to the nearest bed.

Our condition wasn't helped by the experience of getting to our connecting flight at De Gaulle Airport. After deplaning, we found ourselves on the furthest outskirts of the airport with no idea of what to do next. A bus pulled up so everyone, including us, started to get on. I asked the driver if his bus went to terminal 4; he said No so we started to get off. Then someone said to stay on as we had to get a second bus. The bus deposited everyone at a building, where we were herded into an enclosure. Every few minutes a bus would appear at the front of the building and a lady would open the door to let out a few of us. After a while, we made it to the door, were let out and boarded the next bus. This bus, it turned out, did make the rounds of the terminals. There was no announcement of which terminal the bus stopped at but the buildings had numbers on them; we spotted terminal 4, discovered our gate, and we were on our way to Nice. Observation: for American tourists trying to make a connecting flight, De Gaulle Airport leaves something to be desired.

Despite our initial jet lag, we enjoyed our cruise up the Rhone, starting in Aix-en-Provence (I've always wondered where this was) and ending just south of Dijon, where we of course bought some mustard, then proceeded by bus to Paris. Official French-American relations have been somewhat strained, but the residents of the towns we visited along the river were all friendly. The drivers even stopped to let us tourists cross the street (unlike Italy).

All of these French towns had walls dating back to Roman times, churches built in the twelfth century, etc., so the French do have a lot of history and maybe this is one of the reasons they tend to regard us Americans as Johnny-come-lately whippersnappers on the international scene. Perhaps the worst thing from a tourist's standpoint is that the pooper-scooper has not yet made its way into French society so that we had to watch our step, especially in town centers.

One of the most pleasant aspects of French, maybe European, life is sitting in an outdoor café and watching life go by. I observed that no matter what day or what time it was the cafes were always crowded, so I guess somebody else was doing the work. Others have observed that the French economy isn't doing too well and that they'll have to start working longer and harder to be competitive. Whether or not this will reduce the number of café-sitters remains to be seen.

As most tourists know, or soon discover, the French don't believe in serving water or providing napkins. In Paris, we discovered in eating out on our own that at least some restaurants were also inexplicably slow in delivering their food. But for all the little inconveniences of dining out in France the meals, when served, are almost always good. And the French do make good French bread, plus their croissants are the best. So we'll forgive a little tardiness.

One last observation on flying, all of the airlines ask you to get there at least two hours before flight time and, as good American tourists, we always complied. This meant we were always early and ended up spending even more time in airports than we had to. The most interesting example was in returning from Ireland, when we had a 4:15 wake-up call to get there at 5:45, only to find that our airline didn't even open until 6. Yes, I will observe that possibly you don't need to be there two-hours before flight time. And yes, of course once we boarded the Irish airplane we had to sit in it for an hour before it took off. This undoubtedly added to our jet lag, which I'm starting to feel now so will come to a close. Possibly some observations on our Irish experience in future issues.

September 2005 Observations---on the Weather

I ended last month's Observations on Travel by saying I'd have more on our visit to Ireland, but since returning it's been hard to think about anything other than the weather. Longtime area residents will freely admit that it does get kind of warm here during the summer, but, especially when we talk to people from other parts, we like to cite mitigating factors such as the low humidity and the cool nights.

Official promoters of the region go even further. When Beverly and I first moved to Sacramento about 40 years ago, we got a brochure from the Chamber of Commerce saying that the average daily temperature during the summer was around 80 degrees. I think they arrived at this figure by adding the high, 100, and the low, 60, and dividing by two. One summer in Sacramento was enough for us to realize that the Chamber's number was a little low.

Later, when we started looking for a house in Sacramento, the real estate agents would tell us that you really didn't need air-conditioning as it cooled off at night so all you had to do was open up the house. Or they'd tell us that the swamp cooler on the roof, which was a common sight in Sacramento at the time, would do the job. We might have been naïve about a number of things as we looked for our first house but we knew enough to make sure that it had good central air.

Going back to our recent trip for a moment, we stopped in New York on our way to France and Ireland. It was unusually warm for early June, around 80, and very humid. It brought back memories of when I was a kid growing up in New York and what we did to escape the heat (and humidity). Almost every summer, we'd embark on a journey known as "going to the mountains." This meant spending six or seven weeks in July and August in a little bungalow somewhere in the Catskills. Our father would work in the city during the week, then join us on weekends. The bungalow would be small and cramped, the plumbing would be uncertain, there'd be nothing to do there except maybe pick berries and the nearest town would be miles away. But I suppose it was cooler.

During the summers when we didn't go to the mountains, our escape from the heat was to go to Brighton Beach, where my grandparents had a small wooden house. We'd go there just for the day as my grandfather rented out all of the rooms in the house except the small bedroom where he slept. As we lived in the Bronx, we'd get up early, then travel by subway, changing from the IRT to the BMT at 14th Street, for what seemed like hours before finally getting to Brighton Beach. But when we finally got there and emerged from the subway we could breathe in something rare in New York, cool, salty ocean air. When we didn't go to Brighton Beach, the only other escape was to the local movie house, at that time the only place we knew of that was air-conditioned.

So 80 degrees and humid in New York was pretty bad and I told everyone that it might be hotter where we'd come from but it was a dry heat. But let's face it, when it's 107 degrees, dry or not, it's hot, and the effect can be just as enervating as 80 and humid, except that it's like being in a furnace instead of in a steam bath. Let's admit it, this summer has been hot, hot, hot. Luckily, our oldest son David and his wife Laura are taking us to San Francisco this coming weekend for a brief respite from the heat. After that, my plan is to stay indoors where it's nice and air-conditioned until the temperature drops below 100, when it will merely be warm.

October 2005

Another "Observations" on Things Guaranteed to Happen, or TGH's. Another TGH that never fails is that if you make a medical appointment for some day during the winter months there'll be one of our patented storms that day, after weeks of sunshine, and you'll be driving in the wind and rain. The next day will be sunny again.

Okay, time for another Observations on Things Guaranteed to Happen. Readers may recall from prior Observations that Beverly and I went on an extended trip during the month of June. When you go on such a trip, it's guaranteed that you'll miss something, like paying a bill, while you're gone. And, being jet-lagged when you return, you won't remember having missed it until called to account. It's also guaranteed that there'll be something unpleasant, maybe a letter from the Internal Revenus Service, waiting for you in the mail. Plus there'll be at least one ominous-sounding message left on your answering machine.

As we all know, when you're asked if you can do something on a certain date a couple of months down the road you of course say, Sure, no problem, especially when you've been gone for a while and are out of your usual Sun City routine. This is almost a certain guarantee that something will come up, not the day before or the day after, but just on that date, and you'll be left trying to explain your conflict while apologizing and trying to wipe the egg off your face.

Moving on to other Things Guaranteed to Happen that have come to my attention recently---a friend mentioned something I'd also noticed, that when you're driving on a stretch of road, as, say, on Blue Oaks, where two lanes narrow into one, at least one driver will stay in the "passing" lane until the last possible moment, then dart in, expecting you to make way. Of course, we all know about the California turn-off, when (it's guaranteed to happen) some driver, again having waited until the last moment, will cut across two or three lanes to exit from a freeway, regardless of what rest of the traffic is doing. And one more driving Guaranteed to Happen, the safety rule is to stay one car length behind the vehicle in front for every ten miles an hour. So, if you're driving fifty miles an hour and are staying five car lengths behind, what will happen. Right, five cars will immediately cut in front of you.

Some other Things Guaranteed to Happen during the ordinary course of a day. When you go to the bank to make a simple withdrawal or deposit, more often than not the person in front of you has to make a complex financial transaction that seemingly takes hours. Then she (okay, or he, it could be a guy) has to have a little chat with the teller, who's probably a childhood friend, before packing up her (his) papers and finally leaving.

From the bank to the supermarket next door and now you're on the checkout line. If you're in no hurry, then no problem. But if you are in a rush, Guaranteed to Happen, the customer in front of you has some problem with a coupon or a credit card or wants a pack of cigarettes that the checkout person has to go to the back of the store to get.

Finally, in the event of a natural disaster, such as we've recently had in Hurricane Katrina, it's guaranteed that after the initial shock, or even before, that event will be politicized, with the media and the politicians playing the blame game for all it's worth. On the bright side, it's also guaranteed that ordinary people, not politicians or media members, will step up, as Americans always do, to overcome the disaster and move on to recovery.

November 2005 Observations---on Aging

At a meeting I recently attended someone remarked that SCR will be celebrating its tenth anniversary next spring. Is this possible? Seems it was only yesterday that Beverly and I drove out to a dusty spot out in the middle of nowhere with only a sales trailer in view and I predicted that this would never fly.

When Beverly and I moved to SCR almost eight years ago the average age here was about the same as mine, 67. I believe I read somewhere that the average age is now around 73, meaning I've aged more than Sun City. The way I feel, especially my knees, I'm not too surprised.

Needless to say, there've been many changes in and around SCR over the past decade, some good, others not so good. We now have the Galleria (it was a big event when it opened), an Indian casino, countless restaurants, supermarkets, gas stations and other retail outlets, all just a stone's throw away. Of course, we also now have increased traffic, higher prices at those gas stations and road construction all over the place.

I remember the time when you could drive from SCR to the freeway on Blue Oaks with only one stoplight, the one at Foothills. And often you were the only car on the road. Today Blue Oaks has become almost a freeway itself, with trucks rumbling up and down and when the widening is complete I'm sure it'll only get worse. The latest I've heard is that we won't be getting a stoplight at Del Webb and Blue Oaks so we'll have to be vigilant when exiting to avoid becoming a statistic.

I also remember that after moving in we'd walk the streets, often muddy as they were still building, to inspect the neighborhood front yards to see if we could get ideas for our own. Now instead of houses being built there are houses for re-sale, at a price far higher than when we bought. Instead of planting, now we have to prune. After providing a good living to local landscapers and cabinet makers we're now doing the same for local painting companies.

As indicated by my own personal case, as SCR has aged so have its residents. Everyone knows that golf course use has declined, primarily because we don't have as many active golfers. I can testify that there also not nearly as many active tennis players, including myself, those knees again. A few years ago we'd have 12 to 16 players at the morning drop-ins. Nowadays, we're lucky to have four or five. SCR already has a lawn bowling club (although I haven't seen it in action for a while). Maybe we need to have a few shuffleboard courts for shuffling residents. How about a miniature golf course for those who can't make it around a regular golf course any more? It wouldn't be a bad idea to have a few more benches scattered around, either.

One thing about SCR that hasn't changed is the abundance of talented people living here. We have any number of talented artists and crafters and have an outstanding art show every spring plus the annual art sale and boutique coming up early in November. We have a nearly 100-member chorus that puts on great concerts several times a year We have dancers of all kinds and I must mention we also have writers of all kinds.

Sun City was designed as a community for active retirees and although the retirees may be older the community remains active. People volunteer for offices of the many clubs and committees and some even run for places on the Board of Directors. There are as many activities and trips as ever. Or, if you want to take it easy you can browse around the library or keep track of your stocks and bonds in the Wall Street room. And next spring there'll be that 10-year anniversary celebration, which I'm sure will be a gala occasion with all kinds of events, and I'll try to celebrate too even though I'll be another year older.

December 2005 Observations

I'm fond of recollecting those Christmases when I was a kid and the three big presents I received on three successive Christmases: a microscope set, a chemistry set and an erector set. Nowadays I suppose three big presents would be an iPhone, an iPod and a laptop computer.

Observations on Christmases Past

Back in those simpler times when I was a kid (okay, way back) in the Bronx everyone looked forward to Christmas. No school; presents; if it snowed and you were a rich kid with a sled you could ride it in the street; if it snowed and you didn't have a sled you could throw snowballs. Now, as I understand it, in our sophisticated age Christmas has somehow become a controversial issue. You're not supposed to say "Merry Christmas" any more; you can say something like "Happy Holidays," and I'm not even sure about that. And in some places even the colors red and green have been banned. Well, back to these ridiculous antics later. Meanwhile, some memories of Christmases past when Christmas was still Christmas.

Like many readers, I was a kid during the Depression years so our Christmases were pretty minimal. Fortunately, we weren't aware of this. I remember that we used to hang up our stockings on the dumbwaiter (anyone remember those?) handle and on Christmas morning we found possibly an apple and an orange and one toy in them.

Fortunately, again, I had my great aunt and her husband. Since our family (on my mother's side) was Hungarian I knew them as Rizanani and Lazabachi. They lived in a far-off place called Passaic, New Jersey, on the other side of the Hudson River, and so only came to the Bronx once a year, on Christmas. The family met at my grandmother's apartment, where, being Hungarians, they spent the day playing cards. My job was to run down to the corner candy store to get a new deck when needed.

Lazabachi was a barber and even during the Depression people must have needed haircuts because every year he and Rizanani brought my big Christmas present. One year it was a microscope set, the next a science set and then the next year it was the big one, an erector set. My laboratory and workshop was the kitchen table. After supper the table was cleared off and I looked at things through my microscope, mixed liquids in test tubes and built things that actually moved (the erector set had a motor).

When I had my own family and the kids were small my memories are of being awakened early in the morning, actually in the middle of the night, and asked if it was time to open the presents yet. One fond memory is the Christmas when our oldest son, then two, came into our bedroom pulling a wagon filled with ornaments, which he'd carefully removed from the tree (and which we then had to put back on). Other memories involve staying up late on Christmas Eve putting together some toy with directions written in Japanese or Sanskrit.

Then there was the Christmas when we got our youngest son, then eleven, his first computer, called a CoCo (for color computer) from Radio Shack. The computer was set up and then---disaster, the screen kept moving up and down. Out of all the Radio Shack computers available, we'd selected a lemon. Amazingly, a Radio Shack, not the one where we'd bought our computer, was open on Christmas so we sped over there and luckily were able to get another one. It was a harrowing Christmas morning, but the computer investment paid off as our son later became a software engineer.

Well, as stated above, Christmas has become a controversial issue. It seems to me that it's become at once more and more commercial, the hoopla now starting after Halloween (now also a controversial holiday), and is also in increasing danger of losing any religious significance. As I look over what I've written, it seems to me that our Christmases primarily meant family gatherings. These in turn meant kids opening presents, cats playing in the wrapping paper, a fire going in the fireplace, good food, good drink, a wish that something of the Christmas spirit could carry over into the new year. I don't think this will ever change. So Merry Christmas to everyone in Sun City and a Happy New Year.

2006 OBSERVATIONS

January 2006 Observations

A little change in "Observations" looking at the year ahead, this time on what I'd like to see happen in the year 2006. This included decent health coverage for all. Aren't we still wrestling with this in 2010? I also mentioned an energy program that would reduce our dependence on Mideast oil. Don't we still need this in 2010?

What Observations Would Like in 2006

The year 2005 may not rank up there with the best. Hurricanes, earthquakes, famines, the war in Iraq, the 49ers and Raiders having terrible seasons, even the Kings at this writing struggling to get above .500. So let's look ahead to the coming year and outline some of the things Observations would like to see in 2006.

Worldwide: let the nations of the world get together and, if they do nothing else, create a program to eradicate once and for all the diseases that can be eliminated with current medical knowledge. It would be nice if they could also eliminate wars, famines, genocide, dictators, rap singers, phony celebrities and a lot of other bad things, but wiping out diseases than can be dealt with would be a good start and, who knows, might lead to other efforts.

National: let the political parties stop their childish feuding for long enough to agree on a means to provide health coverage to all citizens, at least as good as other industrial nations seem able to provide for their people. And while they're at it, and as long as there is time before the next crisis, come up with a realistic plan to put Social Security on a sound basis. Start, after all these years, an energy program that will cut down on our dependence on Mideast oil. There must be a way; let's figure it out.

Statewide: yes, I know, it's hard to imagine our Legislature accomplishing anything, but as the State's income seems due for a boost, instead of spending it (again) maybe do something that will cut the deficit to a reasonable amount. If they want to spend on something, let them look at our levees and do whatever is needed to make sure our area, if worst comes to worst, doesn't become another New Orleans.

Media and Entertainment: outlaw all TV "news" shows in which two or more "experts" scream at each other. Outlaw all former prosecutors and all defense attorneys who comment on ongoing trials. Ban all "reality" TV shows. Make movies for someone other than teenagers. Reduce the sound in movie theaters to a level less than deafening. Cut out those commercials, which are bad enough on TV; when we go to the movies we want to get away from them. Outlaw all stories on movie stars and other "celebrities" who've been abused as children, who've faced a crisis that's made them better people or who've discovered the meaning of life. Newspapers? I know they're on the way out but still would like to see another one here so it's not just the Sacramento Bee.

Sports: I'd like to see the Kings make the playoffs (think they will despite their slow start). I'd like to see the 49ers and Raiders make comebacks in 2006. Okay, at least one of them. In football, penalize all those linebackers and anyone else who jumps up and down in glee after sacking a poor defenseless quarterback. In basketball, throw anyone who taunts the other team out of the game. Fine Grant Napear $100 every time he says, "And if you don't like that you don't like NBA basketball" or "Put that in the book and send him to the line."

Well, I see this piece is veering in the direction of Life's Little Annoyances, so before I get to what I'd like to see done to Donald Trump, Martha Stewart, Paris Hilton, Tom Cruise and other favorites I'll try to end on a positive note. I'd like to see some of the Christmas spirit (and let's keep the word "Christmas") extend to the new year. Peace on earth and good will to men.

February 2006 Observations

A remembrance of things past, the Automat, well-beloved of everyone who grew up in New York City during the '30's. Going downtown when I was a kid meant eating at the Automat. There was no greater thrill than being given a handful of nickels and then going to those little windows and selecting what you'd have for lunch. I say in the "Observations" below that I still think there's a place for an Automat today, automated of course. Now that we've had our recession I think the argument for bringing back an Automat-type restaurant is even stronger.

Observations on Things Past: The Automat

I was recently talking with some friends about what kinds of restaurants we'd like to see in those new shopping areas going up around us and someone, a New Yorker like me, said, "You know what I'd like, an Automat." This immediately set off a train of memories and we spent the next half-hour reminiscing about the good old days of the Automat.

For readers not acquainted with Automats, these were not restaurants or cafeterias as we know them but eating places, usually large ones and pretty ornate, where you could get food items, set out in glass compartments, by putting nickels into a slot, and something always came out. One of my fondest memories of growing up in New York is being taken to some event downtown, meaning in Manhattan, and then going to eat in the Automat. My mother would give me a handful of nickels, then, all by myself, I'd examine the gleaming compartments filled with enticing things. I'd make my choice, carefully put in the right number of nickels, turn a knob and, lo and behold, the glass door of the little compartment opened and I could take out what I'd selected. Then the compartment would revolve back and forth and, magically, the same item would reappear. What could be neater for a kid?

Out of curiosity, I searched the Web and found an excellent article from the Smithsonian Magazine called "Meet Me at the Automat," which filled in a lot of gaps in what I remembered about eating there. For example, where had all those nickels come from? I know I got them from my mother, but had she saved them up for the occasion? No; to quote from the article, "women with rubber tips on their fingers---'nickel throwers,' as they became known---in glass booths gave customers the five-cent pieces required to operate the food machines in exchange for larger coins and paper money." I must say I have no recollection of this.

I do remember that the food was always good, and the article tells why. "Horn and Hardart Automats had a strict fresh-food policy. No food could be left overnight in any of its restaurants . . . After closing time each day, Horn & Hardart trucks carried surplus food to 'day-old' shops, New York and Philadelphia each had three, located in low-income neighborhoods, which sold these items at reduced prices."

Horn and Hardart? I remember these names now, but who were they? Well, Joseph Horn and Frank Hardart, the latter born in Germany, were the founders of the Automat, which was based on "a successful German eatery." I'd always thought that Automats were a peculiar New York institution and that they'd started maybe in the 1930's as places where people could eat cheaply during the Depression. It turns out that Automats started in Philadelphia in 1902 and then reached Manhattan in 1912.

But how did those food items keep coming out of those compartments? As a child, I simply assumed it was by some kind of magic; as an adult, I was vaguely aware that there must have been people back there. The Smithsonian article says: "The word 'automat' comes from the Greek *automatos*, meaning 'self-acting.' But Automatics weren't truly automatic. They were heavily staffed. As a customer removed a compartment's contents. a behind-the-machine human quickly slipped another sandwich, salad, piece of pie or coffee cake into the vacated chamber."

When I was a kid I didn't drink coffee at the Automat, but when I was older I would stop in for coffee and probably a piece of pie or cake. I now find out that "Horn & Hardart's coffee became known as the best in town. In their heyday in the 1950's, Automats sold more than 90 million cups of fresh-brewed coffee each year. From 1912 to 1950, a cup cost a nickel." I wonder if I stopped drinking Automat coffee after 1950. In any case, the Automat was more or less the Starbuck's of its time. And its coffee was a nickel; hear that, Starbuck's? A nickel.

So, what happened to the Automats, "once the word's largest restaurant chain, serving 800,000 people a day"? The Smithsonian article says: "Automats fell victim to consumers' changing tastes. Perhaps people tired of cafeteria-style food. Many no longer ate a full meal at lunch. Americans moved into the suburbs and didn't come downtown as often, so night business at Automats fell, too." In the 1970s Horn and Hardart replaced its "dying restaurants" with, of all things, Burger King franchises. The last Automat closed in New York City in 1991.

I for one don't think people are tired of cafeteria-style food. The last time we visited New York there were many "fast-food" places, where people lined up to select their dishes. I say let some food entrepreneur put an Automat in Roseville. Maybe to save labor costs robots could be used instead of people to work in back. Retirees could man the hot food counters and change booths. And Automats were a great place to hang out. I'd certainly go there and I'd take my grandchildren, give them a bunch of nickels and let them have a ball.

March 2006 Observations

I see that back in 2006, before the recession, we were worried. I guess you can be worried even when things aren't going that bad. I think I made an acute observation, that the current generation had a need to feel connected. Some guys invented Facebook and Twitter and cashed in on this observation. This commentary on the technological revolution and its effects on us came even before the iPhone and the iPad. Now I'm really worried.

I've been reading recently that there's a general feeling of worry in the country. The reasons most cited are the war in Iraq, the economy, and possibly the fear that Dennis Rodman will return to NBA basketball. This is the kind of assertion that's impossible to verify, or not verify. Maybe the writers themselves are worrying because the newspapers or magazines they write for are going to be replaced by internet blogs. .

If anything is making me uneasy nowadays, except for still another Rocky film, it's the feeling that I'm being left high and dry by the latest wave of the technological revolution. A little over a year ago my wife Beverly and I bought a digital camera. We can now take pictures with it, transfer the pictures to a computer and then print them out. We can even e-mail them to other people. I thought that, aha, we'd caught up.

Then the other day Beverly asked me what an Ipod was and I realized that I didn't really know. The other day our soon- to-be-obsolete newspaper had a story about the Blackberry (not the fruit but the thing). Beverly asked me what a Blackberry was and again I didn't really know. Well, we know what to do when you want to find out what something is; right, we go to Google.

From what Google told me, I gather that an iPod (not Ipod) is a small device that fits into one's pocket and was originally designed to play music. One of the articles I read said the iPod can hold up to 15,000 songs. But iPod uses, like those of cell phones, have expanded. They can also hold up to 150 hours of video on a 2 ½ inch screen. You can also watch videos bought from the iTunes Music Store. No, I don't know what that is but I'd guess it's on the Web.

Okay, now, my question is: do we really need to have 15,000 songs in our pocket, and do we really want to watch video on a 2 ½ inch screen? I know I don't. If I want to listen to music I prefer to do it at home, on a tape, a CD or even a phonograph, an old-fashioned device that plays records (does anyone nowadays know what these are?). As for that 2 ½ inch screen, I wouldn't be able to tell Oprah from Dr. Phil (or are they the same?)

The BlackBerry (correct spelling, I think), it's a handheld PDA devise that's engineered for e-mail. Most models have a built in mobile phone. So I guess if you're away from your computer you can send and receive e-mail with a BlackBerry. My question: isn't it bad enough getting all those junk e-mails on your regular computer? Who needs to carry around something so they can follow you wherever you are? Oh, yes, PDA stands for personal digital assistant.

So now I know what an iPod and a BlackBerry are, and even know how to spell them. Where does this leave us, or me? Well, I guess I'm more knowledgeable about the latest gadgets but I have another worry. When you add the iPods and BlackBerries to those ubiquitous cell phones, I see a generation that can't stand not to be connected. This generation has to hear its music, watch its videos, get its emails and talk to each other all the time, 24/7. If they're worried, maybe it's not so much about Iraq or the economy as fearing they'll be cut off, out of the loop, left alone. On second thought, I'll stop worrying about them as it won't do any good anyway, let the pundits figure it all out and go back to taking pictures with our digital camera.

April 2006 Observations

Sun City Roseville was going to celebrate its tenth anniversary at the end of April 2006 so I thought it appropriate to do another "Observations" on the current state of our retirement community. I noted that it was now settled down but that the spirit of togetherness we had at the beginning, when streets were still muddy and houses were going up and everyone had similar problems, was fraying a little. I suppose that this is inevitable for any place.

Observations After Almost Ten Years in Sun City

As everyone should know by now, Sun City Roseville will be celebrating its tenth anniversary with a week-long series of events at the end of this month. Beverly and I were not among the first hardy settlers as, when we came out, saw the trailer in the middle of an empty field and observed no life forms except jackrabbits, coyotes and Del Webb salespersons, I said, "This place will never fly." But, a couple of years later, I gave in, told Beverly, "Okay, if you guarantee that we'll be ten minutes from a shopping mall, ten minutes from an Indian casino and 10 minutes from a Krispy Crème doughnut place, I'll consider it," and so here we are.

As indicated above, lots of things have changed about SCR, but some things have stayed the same. In my first Observations, about eight years ago, I observed: the parking lot at the Lodge is always filled with cars but when you go into the Lodge it's almost empty. Where did all the people go? After all this time, I still haven't gotten a satisfactory answer. If anyone knows, it's Dodie and she isn't talking.

I also observed that everyone in SCR likes to eat and this led, in a way, to my doing Favorite Restaurants. I know this is still true because people are always asking and telling me about restaurants. A few times I've thought Favorite Restaurants had reached the end of the line because they couldn't possibly build more places to eat around here. As in my original prediction about SCR, I was wrong. There seems to be no limit to the number of eating places coming to our area and, with more and more developments being started, it seems that Favorite Restaurants will be around for a while.

Another early SCR observation, which still holds, was that it you get to any event here on time you're already too late. There seems to be something about our generation that makes us fearful of missing something, being left out, or being told, Sorry, we've just let in the last one. If you're planning to attend any of the tenth anniversary events, and we all should, keep this in mind.

As for the changes in SCR itself, I remember that when we first moved here, to Village 2, they were still building, the streets were muddy, it was noisy, Del Webb people were always rushing around, it was a hectic time. It was also kind of fun because everyone was pretty much in the same boat. Everyone had some kind of problem and the neighbors all had advice on what to do about it. People were out on the street, everyone said "Hello," exchanged information on where they were from, discussed their houses, their landscaping, their appliances and everything else. Now the streets aren't muddy, it's generally quiet and things have settled down, but you don't see that many people outside any more and some (not many) even go by without so much as a wave.

In my first Observations, I said: whenever two people at Sun City meet and find they find something in common they form a club. This was only a slight exaggeration. I believe there are as many clubs or groups here now as there ever was, maybe more. But I've heard that it's becoming harder to find people willing to become officers, i.e., to do the work, and this is possibly also true of the various Sun City committees. This is understandable, we're all getting older, some even ten years older. Maybe a tenth anniversary celebration will inspire a new spirit of togetherness and of participation. Certainly everyone at the celebration events will say "Hello" to one another.

At various times I've observed here on the things that made Beverly and I glad we moved to Sun City. Just off the top of my head, I'll list: the Lodge, the Timbers restaurant, the library, the pool room (since I've taken this up), the Singers, the fitness center, the pool, the events, the trips, the Galleria, all the eating places and stores on Fairway Drive; more importantly, the Sun City staff (who've worked so hard to put this anniversary celebration together), the friends we've made here, the help we've always gotten from our neighbors.

I wrote eight years ago: Sun City Roseville residents don't only eat, travel, cruise and form clubs. There are many admirable people here who volunteer to help others. They drive, visit, take food to sick neighbors, provide support, raise funds and donate. This is still true today. Okay, see you all at the anniversary celebration.

May 2006 Observations—on Cruising and Other Stuff :

Observations has commented on the pleasures and perils of cruising before so I won't devote this entire space to our recent Mexican Riviera experience. I do, however, have to once again observe that cruise passengers, who I'm sure can find their way about on shore, seem to become confounded once they board the ship. From the first day to the last, people would wander around, asking if this was the way to the dining room or to the theater or to this or that lounge. Luckily, a cruise ship, no matter how large, does have boundaries and nobody was reported as having fallen overboard so I assume that sooner or later most found what they were looking for. The ship's elevators in particular continually baffled passengers. They would get onto our elevator going down and express amazement that it wasn't going up. The same was true when the elevator was going up and they wanted to go down. How to explain this curious phenomenon? It must have to do with something being displaced when people leave the real world and enter the cruise world.

Just one more observation on cruises. It seems that the cruise lines feel they have to provide their passengers with as many activities as for the kids at a summer camp. So throughout the day there's a constant stream of such things as demonstrations of fruit and vegetable carvings, trivia games, fun word games, and of course bingo. My question is: do people want to pay for a cruise just so they can do such things? And what about the man I observed spending hours on the library computer playing solitaire? Is this why he came on a cruise? Well, maybe it's just to pass the time in-between meals.

Anyway, it's back to the usual routine and as always the cruise experience, since it's so unreal, quickly fades like a dream. Those daily five-course meals where the waiters wanted to serve you three desserts and those cabins, pardon me, staterooms, which the steward always saw to it were neat when you returned, no matter how messy when you left, are but distant memories. So, what's going on now? Somehow, when you're gone, even for a short time, you expect things to change, but as usual nothing much seemed to happen while we were gone.

Bush was still president; he hadn't been impeached yet. Iraq was still Iraq. The Republicans and Democrats in Washington hadn't done anything meaningful; neither had the Republicans and Democrats in Sacramento. People were protesting all over the world. The same people on television were still saying the same old things. But "24" was still on and Jack Bauer was still saving the country while everyone else on the show was being killed off, even Edgar. (Where do you march to protest that?) The Kings were still fighting for a playoff berth. Sports Illustrated had an excerpt from a book detailing Barry Bonds performance-enhancing drug use, but didn't we all, except possibly the baseball commissioner, know about that? The same old mail was waiting for us: bills and solicitations for credit cards or money. The same old spam was on the computer. It was still raining.

But despite our wet weather, spring is officially here and eventually, as we know, we'll be having warm (and hot) sunny Valley days that even our weather forecasters will be able to predict. Rain or shine, the baseball season opens in a week and that's always good, despite all attempts to ruin the game. "The Sopranos" are back and maybe everyone will be killed off by the final episode. By the time this appears, SCR's tenth anniversary celebration will be over and we'll be heading into our 11ᵗʰ year, if that's believable. Sometime soon my book will be coming out---wait, that's for next issue.

On the cruise, I read P.D. James's latest mystery (available in the SCR library). I mention this because she's 86 years old and still going strong. We also saw the latest "Pride and Prejudice" film on the cruise (for free, except for paying for the cruise) and it was very good (better than "Brokeback Mountain", that Jane Austen was really a good screenwriter) so maybe there's hope for the movies. Well, that's the back-from-the-cruise column. Coming up: books we read as kids (anyone remember John R. Tunis and Paul Gallico?), comic strips (Terry and the Pirates) and maybe radio, TV shows and movies in those good old pre-historic days

June 2006 Observations

The "Observations" below was about books I'd remembered reading as a kid, books by such writers as John R. Tunis, Paul Gallico and Edgar Rice Burroughs (Tarzan). Somehow nothing that came after was ever as enjoyable as these early experiences. I can still recall the covers of other books, Treasure Island and Robinson Crusoe among them, with their elaborate colored illustrations, invitations to worlds of excitement and adventure. I think this "Observations" is especially pertinent today, when it seems that traditional books may be on the way out, to be replaced by devices such as Kindle. I hope this never happens. (Note: Apple's iPad is about to come out).

In last month's Sun Senior News, I said I'd be writing about books we read when we were kids. There was something about those early reading experiences that could never be duplicated: learning about people and things beyond our little childhood life; getting caught up in adventure and mysteries; discovering a new author we liked, finding more of his (or her) books in the library and looking forward to reading them when we got home. The first books we read may not have been classics, although some were, but they generated an excitement that later books couldn't match and after all these years still stick in our minds.

Elsewhere in this issue, I have an article announcing that a book of short stories I've written and self-published is now out and available to Sun City readers. In one of these stories,

I say, as a kind of nod to someone whose books I still remember fondly, that the hero's favorite writer (the hero is 12 years old) is John R. Tunis. (See how cleverly I've worked that in). As a kid, I read a lot of sports books, most of which were probably juvenile mush, with the all-American hero triumphing in the end over some dastardly villain or villains. Tunis's books stood out, I think, because, even to a kid, they had a ring of truth to them.

The first book of his I read was called "The Kid from Tompkinsville," and although the hero started out as an all-winning pitcher, bang, right in the middle of the story, he hurt his arm, and had to come back as a hitter. If this sounds familiar, right, it's very similar to the plot of "The Natural," the book written by Bernard Malamud which was made into the movie with Robert Redford, and I wouldn't be surprised if Mr. Malamud had also read "The Kid from Tompkinsville" when he was young. The hero of "The Natural," by the way, is Roy Hobbs; of "The Kid," Roy Tucker.

Nowadays you can look up anything on the Internet, so I looked up John R. Tunis and wasn't surprised to find he'd been a sportswriter for the New York Evening Post from 1925-32; no wonder his accounts of sporting events seemed authentic. I also saw that he'd gone to Harvard and to Boston University Law School, so he was no dummy. He also served in France during World War II. He was born in 1889 and died in 1975: I was happy that he'd had a long life.

The name Paul Gallico (1897-1976), may be more familiar than that of Tunis. Like Tunis, Gallico was a sports writer, in fact was sports editor of the New York Daily News and invented and organized the Golden Gloves (that's from the Internet again). He sold a short story to the movies for $5,000 in 1936, went to Europe and became a novelist, writing over 40 books, including "The Snow Goose" and "The Poseidon Adventure." I'm sure most readers have heard of that last one.

I remember Gallico for a book he wrote just after he quit his sportswriter job. It's appropriately called "Farewell to Sports" and I still have my paperback copy, an original pocket book put out during World War II and costing 25 cents. Yes, times have changed. "Farewell to Sports" is still worth looking into for its honest look at sports, including their more unsavory aspects, plus its description of Gallico as a young man getting into the ring with Jack Dempsey.

Gallico was an early George Plimpton. Like Tunis, he went to a prestigious college, Columbia, served in World War II, and had a relatively long, and certainly very productive, life.

Well, besides a salute and a thank-you to Mssrs. Tunis and Gallico, I wanted to mention a few of the other writers I enjoyed as a kid, Edgar Rice Burroghs, of course, for his Tarzan books, H.G. Wells for his early sci-fi novels and a writer named Clarence E. Mulford (1883-1956), who wrote the Hopalong Cassidy books, on which all of those William Boyd movies we saw as kids were based.

I realize I've been talking about books read by boys so I asked my wife Beverly what she read when she was young and she remembers the Bobbsey Twins, the Nancy Drew mysteries, "My Friend Flicka" and other stories by Mary O'Hara, and books about Silver Chief, an Alaskan sled dog, by Jack O'Brien. The internet reveals interesting facts about these writers, such as that the Nancy Drew books, started by Carolyn Keene, were written by a number of authors. More later, I hope. .

July 2006 Observations---on Work

In the last couple of issues Observations has gone down memory lane and it's tempting to take still another trip down there. But I feel the need (and maybe readers do, too) for a change of pace, so this month Observations is taking a look (backwards) at something most of us were involved in, remember, work.

I'd guess that when I retired from being a research analyst with the State (of California) 15 ½ years ago my experiences were typical of many readers. In the first few months after I left I received phone calls from my office, visited there and Beverly and I were even taken to dinner by my agency head for some work I came in to do. Then the phone calls and visits gradually stopped. After a while when I did stop in I didn't recognize most of the people there, and they didn't recognize me. Finally, my old job faded into the past and I took on my new "job," being retired.

It's been so long ago now that I'd pretty well forgotten everything about my State job and the only time I thought about work at all was when I'd hear an early-morning traffic report on the radio and think how glad I was no longer to be out there in the commute. What started me thinking about work recently was hearing about the travails of the office place from some of my younger acquaintances. Ah, yes, I thought, I remember all that.

There were all of those office types so brilliantly depicted by Scott Adams in his comic strip Dilbert: the pointy-headed oblivious boss focused on his own concerns, chief of which was looking good to his boss; the back-stabber who was your best friend to your face but wait until he (or she) talked to your boss when you weren't around; the shirker who never seemed to be around when a big job came up and whose work everyone else would have to do. Well, you know all of these types and more.

As I worked for the State, the most common type of manager was the one who was deathly scared of rocking the boat. I wonder how many times I heard, "But that's the way we've always done things (ineptly) here"? And being the State, there was the constant interchange of memos, which I suppose were meant to indicate you were on the job, while accomplishing nothing. Above all, there were the meetings. Staff meetings had to be held at least weekly, even if there was nothing to discuss. Then there were Division and Agency meetings in which so many people were involved, each pushing his (or her) own agenda that they were guaranteed to produce nothing. In fact, I don't ever recall being in a meeting that actually resulted in anything being done.

Okay, maybe I'm painting too bleak a picture of my work experience. I don't like to think it was all for nothing and I believe I did accomplish some things, but not by exchanging memos or going to meetings. One thing I'm sure I did. I was in charge of a survey asking State employees to rate their health plans, a survey nobody else seemed to think important, and now when I get my health plan information every year there's a questionnaire asking about my use and satisfaction. So somebody up there caught on.

Work, while often frustrating, did provide life with a certain structure (as well as a paycheck) and, again, I think, like most people, I missed that structure when I retired. Looking back though, on the whole I'm not sorry I left when I did. Pointy-headed bosses, back-stabbers and all the rest, I'll gladly leave those to the younger generation. I'm too old for such stuff. I mentioned above taking on the "job" of being retired. Next month some Observations on this.

August 2006 Observations---on Retirement

In last month's Observations I described what may be a typical experience when retiring from a job. For the first few months I was called and called my old office and, when downtown, visited my old fellow workers. Then, as time went on, the calls and visits dwindled and finally came to a stop. I was then left to turn to the "job" of retiring.

Work, as noted last month, whatever else it is, provides a structure for your life. I wonder how many readers dreaded the moment when you'd wake up in the morning and, without a job to go to, wonder: What do I do for the rest of the day? I have to admit this thought crossed my mind more than once after I retired.

So, what did I do? For the first few months, I caught up on my sleep, discovering that it wasn't natural after all to get up at 6:30 every morning. Getting up at 9:30 or 10 left a much shorter day to fill. I also caught up on chores around the house and in the yard. I finally fixed that broken sprinkler. Or maybe I called someone to fix it; I can't really remember. I fixed up the room that used to be my oldest son's, now off to college, as an office. I installed a computer; or rather, my youngest son hooked it up for me. But there came a time when I was all caught up Now what?

I think I did what many retirees do; I raced around to find things to fill up my time. I volunteered. I signed up for a class. I joined a couple of senior organizations. I started writing for an alternative weekly newspaper. Before I knew it, my time was almost as booked up as when I was working, some days even more so. Wait a minute, I thought, is this really why I retired? So I reassessed the situation, cut down on or cut out some activities and left enough "free" time to do other things, or sometimes just nothing.

One of the things demanded by work is that you have to be at a certain place at a certain time, especially when you work for the State. I never particularly liked this so I tried to cut out such activities or at least keep them to a minimum. Last month I mentioned all of the countless meetings I attended, which never resulted in anything. So I try not to go to meetings, although sometimes at Sun City these can't be avoided. I tried to leave time so that I and my wife Beverly could just say, Why don't we go out to lunch today, or to dinner, or to the movies, or to the Galleria? I like what I think of as "retirement" days, when I have nothing scheduled at all. I might go to the library or to a bookstore and browse around, without having to worry about the time.

As readers know, having found an avocation in writing I didn't give it up, and in this I was lucky. Being a free-lance writer does mean you have to talk to people, but I could set my own time for an interview (if okay with the interviewee, of course) and do my writing when I wanted, during the day or at night. Also, if I didn't want an assignment I didn't have to take it. Too bad I couldn't do that when I was working.

This doesn't mean that I have the "job" of retirement all figured out. After 15 ½ years, I'm still working on it. Maybe in another 15 ½ years, if I'm still around, I'll have it almost all figured out.

September 2006 Observations---on Homecomings

One of the themes of British author C.P. Snow, and the title of one of the novels in his series "Strangers and Brothers," was "Homecoming." As I recall, Lewis Eliot, the hero of the series, comes home as a child to find bad news, a family bankruptcy, I think, rather than a death, and from then on fears what he'll find when returning home. I share this fear and remember that when returning to our old house in Carmichael after a trip, especially when we'd left our teen-aged sons at home, when we turned the corner and drove up our street, I'd always say, "Well, at least the house is still standing."

Beverly and I recently returned to Sun City after a trip back East. Our travel day back went like clockwork: the bellman arrived at our room at the exact specified time; when we arrived with our luggage in the lobby the driver of our airport van was there to greet us; there was no traffic tie-up as feared on the way to the airport (we were leaving from Boston and because one of the Big Dig tunnels had been closed we'd been warned of this). When we arrived in Sacramento a Super Shuttle van was ready to leave. On the drive to Sun City, I couldn't help think that things had gone so smoothly something bad was bound to be waiting for us, that was in addition to the heat, which we'd read about and expected.

Sure enough, when we pulled up to our house we saw our cat sitter's van in our driveway and when we came in there she was, on the hallway floor, trying to repel a long line of invading ants. The ants were coming in from the garage, through the laundry room, then the hallway into the kitchen. We figured they wanted to get out of the heat into someplace that was cool. Fortunately, our pest control person from Clark (yes, we called and said, Clark we need you, and how) came the next morning and, as far as we can tell, the big ant invasion is over, at least for now.

The ant event led me to think about homecomings in past years. In one case, our teenage sons had evidently had a party in our house while we were away, against our specific instructions, of course. We heard from our neighbors after that one. At other times, it seems that something had happened to one or another of our sons' cars in our absence so the first thing I had to do was make a trip to the auto repairman, not my choice while still jet-lagged. At another time, our washing machine had overflowed. It turned out that one of our sons had overloaded it, a relief in a way, since the machine was okay, but a mess to clean up.

There were undoubtedly other unwanted events at other homecomings. Despite all this, I find it's always a relief to finally return home after a trip and the older I get the more I feel this way. Beverly and I like to travel and it's always nice to have a change of scenery, see new places, meet new people. But you can only travel for so long, getting on and off the tour bus, packing and unpacking your bags; or, on a cruise, eating those fattening meals three times a day. So it's always nice when our plane lands at Sacramento airport, we take the van, or sometimes a taxi, it pulls into Sun City, there it is, our house, still standing, and it's especially nice that our cats, Shandyman and Bun-Bun, will be there waiting for us.

October 2006 Observations

The spam never ends. I'm still getting e-mails telling me I've won this or that lottery and e-mails from people with names I associate with the Taliban asking me to urgently reply. Occasionally, I still wonder who these people are and why they send these e-mails. On the whole, I've come to accept them as a part of our computer-centered life and routinely delete their e-mails before going on with my other computer tasks.

Observations on E-Mails I Never Read

As with junk mail, we all get our daily dose of spam; it's the price we pay for using computers. In the past few months I've started making notes on some of the spam-mails I've received. No, I haven't had many trying to get me to buy stuff to enhance my sexual prowess, although one of my favorite New Yorker cartoons shows a man replying to such an e-mail, thanking them for their concern but saying he was satisfied with the way he was.

But I've had lots of similar unsolicited stuff. Before the housing slump, I had a lot of spam-mails advising me of low interest rates. More recently, Rolex watches seem to have become the product of the day. It's amazing how many people have these to sell. I can, if I wished, also get incredibly low-cost medicines. I guess these spammers know how expensive medicines have become and want to capitalize on a good thing.

Of course, I've been the lucky winner of many lotteries, the Australian, the South African, the Nigerian, the Brazilian, maybe even the Iranian. Why can't I be that lucky when I go to Thunder Valley? An e-mail I couldn't help looking at was that one from an African bank official informing me that I was heir to several million dollars. There were some complications, but if I sent this bank official a certain amount of money he'd cut through all of the red tape and see to it that I received my rightful inheritance. What a great guy!

A number of the e-mails have interesting, if somewhat baffling, subjects. One said simply: "We never repent of having eaten too little." The sender was a Mr. Holman Andrea. Maybe Mr. Andrea is a reader of my "Favorite Restaurants" column. Another e-mail, from a Marie Keen, had as its subject: "LOL." I wonder if that referred to "little old ladies"? The subject of an e-mail from Elvirat McKeeplu was the cryptic: "Code #WA468." Now what was that about? An e-mail from Ivan Barnes asked "What is OEM software and why do you care?" I have no idea what OEM software is and the truth is that I don't really care. Lisa Wong wrote: "Fun, peach-colored." That was intriguing, although I'm not sure what peach-colored fun is and probably don't want to know.

Some of my spammers have had my e-mail address recommended to them by family members. Mr. Jerald Karser said: "My Spouse Recommended this Site to Me." Mr Fair, no first name, said: "My niece recommended this site to me." The subjects of other e-mails are really baffling. For example, that of a message from Tau Domenico, was "woqep" and that of a message from Sohor Travino was the equally mysterious "eylar." Oh, yes, here's another, from Xun Somers, "dyruc." At times, the spammers seem to have gotten together. Just recently, I had e-mails from Sandy Wyatt, Larry Cody and Ronda Chaney, all with the subject: "uh oh."

Any number of these spammers were anxious to have me respond to their messages. Dramhed usman said: "URGENT RESPOND NEEDED!!!" Diego Seahn said: "Trusting to hear from you Immediately." A few were friendly, such as one from Eloise Shaw: "what up man loanesss." I'm not sure what that last word means, possibly something to do with loans, although whether offering or wanting one is not clear.

Alert readers may have observed that most of these spammers have unusual names, not just John Smith or Bob Jones. Many sound as if they're from a list of likely terrorists. Some examples: Sharif Nahil, Aishuto Mohammed and Hashim Coates. The spelling and grammar of these people is also not always impeccable. The e-mail telling me I'd won the Euromillion Lottery, said: "Remenber to State Yr Winning Info's." Kate faustina wrote: "Vacancy with High Salary and crying and converged on." That vacancy with high salary sounded okay, but I'm not sure if I like the "crying" part and I certainly don't want to be "converged on." Then there's the e-mail from Valare Michaud with the long subject, saying: "Instrumentation shiver baueri aeneid Bennett decontrolling rose morirty deliex." If anyone has any idea of what that's all about, please let me know. And one more question about these spam-mails: do the people who send them actually think anyone will open them, much less read them and reply to them? Well, enough for the spammers; I have to go look and see what junk there is in the regular, or snail, mail.

November 2006 Observations--- Looks Anew at LLAs

It's been a while since Observations has looked at Life's Little Annoyances (LLAs), but they're still out there waiting to get you. Recently, Beverly's laptop gave her a warning that her old phone access number to get on the internet was being discontinued, something that's annoying enough when all you want to do is take a look at your e-mail.

The computer listed some numbers to replace the old one and warned that we should check to make sure these were local ones so we didn't have to pay long-distance charges. So I called our local phone company and this led to more annoyance. My call was answered by a computer which gave me the usual options, none of which seemed to fit our needs. So I took a chance and punched one and again received the usual computer options plus the option of waiting to talk to a human being, none of whom was available right now because they were servicing other hapless callers like me. After a wait of some 20 minutes, I finally got to a human being, who amazingly was able to tell me the phone numbers were indeed local.

Okay, back to the laptop and there followed a series of instructions, none of which led to a place where I could somehow enter the new phone number. So I took Beverly's cell phone, an annoying device in itself as it has a habit of going dead in the middle of important calls, and dialed, ha ha, technical assistance. I was put through to, no surprise, a person with an Indian accent. I explained my situation, saying it was a simple matter, all I wanted to know was how to replace the old obsolete phone number with a good new one. After assuring me he could help, he proceeded to ask me questions for some five minutes---my name, phone number, address, the laptop's operating system, etc., etc.---then said he was transferring me to someone else. At this point, I'd had enough, said Thank You and hung up. There went the morning. Annoying? Yes.

Another recent event. Going to the bank is almost certain to be annoying. Our particular bank never seems to have enough tellers available, the customers in line ahead of me always seem to have complicated transactions (never a simple deposit or withdrawal), the tellers are all youngsters who are overly friendly to senior citizens (Hi, Martin, how's it going?) On this occasion, I had a fairly large check to deposit and a small check to cash.

To deposit the large check, I had to wait for the teller to get approval from a supervisor, who of course was on a lengthy phone call. When it came to the small check deposit, I had to swipe my ATM card, which I hardly ever use except on trips. Then I had to give my PIN, which I'd forgotten, so I told the teller I'd just deposit it. Then I asked for my balance and, after depositing two checks, still had to show an ID. Why? The teller said, anyone could come into the bank and ask for my balance. Sure, after depositing two checks. Well, you can't be too careful. But it's pretty annoying.

Having to show an ID brings me to an old LLA but I'll mention it once more because the longer it goes on the more annoying it gets. This is of course the airport experience. I've been hoping that after all these years airport screening would become more sensible, but not a chance. On a recent trip, an elderly lady was pulled over and had her tweezers confiscated. Well, no elderly lady with tweezers is going to take over any of our airplanes. I was a little annoyed when on our return from Europe last year, having been forced to take four separate flights, I had to take my shoes off four times. The fourth time, after we'd been traveling about 20 hours, almost sent me over the edge but I told myself, at least you can be sure that no 75-year-old terrorist is going to get through with explosives in his shoes.

Okay, that's enough LLAs for now. We're planning to get a new laptop and maybe going broadband or DSL, which means we'll be dealing with our local phone companies again, a surefire recipe for more of LLAs. Stay tuned.

December 2006 Observations

As most readers already know, the current hot issue in Sun City Roseville, is the SPU2 Report, which proposes some major renovations here at considerable cost. The proposals stirred up enough interest so that over 1,000 residents came to a special Board meeting on the subject. Observations will withhold comment on SPU2, but I'd like to throw out a few modest proposals which would, I think, have a reasonable cost, and improve the quality of life in our community.

First, I've mentioned here a few times previously that SCR seems to have skimped on putting benches here. Walking is recommended as one of the best, if not the best, exercises for seniors, but as seniors, and as we become older seniors, it would be nice to have an occasional bench on which to sit and rest. I don't think the cost of a few additional benches would be exorbitant and I believe this would benefit many of our residents. (Incidentally, I've been told that SCLH has more benches than SCR).

One of the places that could use an additional bench or two is Schoolhouse Park, which at present has only one. A park with only one bench; somehow, that just doesn't seem right. And speaking of Schoolhouse Park, I remember when it was opened with great fanfare and since then, as far as I know, has rarely been used. The main reason for this, of course, is the lack of restroom facilities. As I recall, the reason for no facilities was the fear of transients using them. The result has been that almost nobody in SCR uses the park.

Maybe it's already been done, but why not at least look into the possibility of putting restrooms in Schoolhouse Park, see whose permission has to be granted and what the cost would be. Anything that can be done to make this park a better amenity for SCR would be a step in the right direction.

What other modest improvements would benefit SCR? Well, every cruise I've been on has had shuffleboard and this is a standard activity for seniors. So why not a shuffleboard court, and why not put in a horseshoe court (is it a court?) along with it. Where to put these? Well, Schoolhouse Park has a lot of space in it.

Another thing that's occurred to me is not a physical amenity but an event. I recall that when we first moved to SCR there seemed to be lots of community-wide events that attracted everyone and gave residents a chance to meet with one another. Then there was this year's Ten-Year Anniversary celebration, which did the same thing. I know how much work went into the Anniversary events, but maybe we can have a more modest community-wide anniversary event every year. The Association can provide refreshments to draw people; the clubs can have tables to recruit new members; maybe Board members and staff can be there to talk (and listen to) people in an informal setting.

Okay, these are just the thoughts of one SCR resident. To put this on a more scientific basis, there could be a survey asking residents in general what modest and relatively inexpensive improvements they'd suggest to make SCR a better place. Oh, I almost forgot the suggestion made by Sid Salinger, who spends every summer day at the outside pool: young ladies to fan those reclining on their beach chairs and to also bring cool drinks. Uh, just kidding, although this might not be a bad idea, and Sid says that adding some small tables to that area would be helpful.

One more thing that occurred to me: more comfortable chairs for events taking place in the ballroom and also at Sierra Pines. And maybe, considering the many events held there, something can be done to make Sierra Pines a more welcoming place

2007 OBSERVATIONS

January 2007 Observations

The "Observations" below was inspired by the obscene payments to entertainers, athletes, rock stars and the like. I know that putting a cap on such payments, as suggested, will never be done, but I still think it's a good idea. President Obama agrees with me, with regard to bankers anyway. If anything, such payments have become even more obscene in the last few years. Maybe there'll be a tipping point sometime in the future.

Observations Solves (most of) the Nation's Problems

In last year's Observations I listed some of the things I'd like to see happen in 2006. For example, I wrote that I'd like to see health insurance for everyone, an attempt to tackle our looming Social Security deficit before it became a crisis, and a ban on all television "reality" shows. None of these happened; in fact, none of the things I listed came to pass with the exception of the Sacramento Kings making the playoffs (and this was pretty close).

So this time around, instead of a wish list for 2007 which is doomed to failure, Observations will offer a simple way of solving many of our nation's problems. Let's start by going back to those Sacramento Kings. The players on the Kings make a lot of money, as do the owners, who would like to have the tax-payers foot the bill for a new arena. The players on all NBA teams make a lot of money, as do all major league sports players, football, baseball, hockey and the rest. In today's sports section, there's a report that the New York Yankees have offered over $26 million just for the chance of signing a Japanese pitcher, this after the Boston Red Sox offered $51.1 million for the chance of signing another Japanese pitcher. Have things gotten out of hand here? What do you think?

I know what my wife Beverly thinks. Every time she sees a news item about some sports figure, or some entertainment figure, or some big business mogul, who's getting an obscene amount of money she says there should be a law against this. So I hereby propose Beverly's law putting a cap on payments to any individual. Let's make it reasonable; say, a million dollars, so anyone can still aspire to this amount.

The first question is: are there enough of these obscenely paid people so that such a cap would be meaningful? Well, in the NBA, NFL, NHL and MLB alone, there are 123 teams. Figuring an average of 20 on a team and an average salary of $5 million, this comes to over $12 billion. By my standards, this is quite a bit of money. I don't know how many obscenely-paid entertainers are out there (some might say they all are), plus TV anchorpersons who just read the news, media moguls, executives like those at Enron, star college professors who don't teach, etc., etc. But let's say at a conservative estimate there are 50,000 of them averaging $5 million. This makes $250 billion a year.

So, instead of throwing away $250 billion a year, what can be done with this money? For one thing, maybe we can see to it that every citizen in this country has decent health care. And if this is done, is it possible that a healthier populations would save more billions of dollars? I'd say so. Then there's the question of shoring up Social Security. Maybe this too can be addressed. That would take care of two things on my wish list for 2006.

In addition to all this surplus money, now wasted, that could be put to good use, there'd by many other nice results coming from this proposal. No more breathless stories as the one noted above about athletes being offered ridiculous sums of money. Maybe ticket prices to sports events would be lowered (they should) and average families could afford to go to games without mortgaging their houses. No more breathless stories about anchorpersons being offered ridiculous amounts to read the news. No more tales of entertainment figures with their expensive cars, houses, retinues and silly doings. No more outrageous payments and perks to big corporations executives.

Well, you can undoubtedly think of many more good things resulting from ending these obscene payments to people, most of whom in no way deserve such rewards, and when athletes and entertainers, CEOs and CFOs, doctors and lawyers and the like are forced to subsist on no more than a million a year maybe ordinary people will be able to earn more

Meanwhile, for 2007, I'd still like to see the Kings make the playoffs again, although I'd like it more if they weren't paid all that money and if their multi-millionaire owners hadn't made that Carl's Jr. commercial. Happy new year; maybe it'll be better.

February 2007 Observations

I see by the "Observations" below that the iPhone came out three years ago. As we now know, it was a phenomenal success and just recently the iPad was introduced. So the electronic enhancement of our lives continues. I've since seen an actual iPhone and was impressed by all of its many applications. I also see that Steve Jobs said that having an iPhone was like having your life in your pocket. Maybe so, but I'm not so sure that I want to have my life in my pocket. What if somebody picked my pocket?

The start of a new year (I'm writing this on January 10) is the traditional time to look back reflectively on the year just ended and perhaps also to look ahead to what might be coming. I was thinking of doing this but by the time this Observations appears it will be February and that's kind of late; besides, hundreds of reflections and predictions will have already come out. Instead, since my birthday happens to almost coincide with the start of the year I thought I'd look back at some of the changes that have taken place during my (and, for most Sun Cityites, our) lifetimes.

Since this morning's newspaper has announced the unveiling of something called the iPhone, let's consider the telephone and what's happened to it in the past 70 years or so. I must have been five or six when my family had its first telephone and I can't remember exactly what it looked like, but I'm sure it was large, cumbersome, had a dial and a receiver you picked up and it was black. We didn't get many phone calls but when the phone rang it was an important event. Because people didn't make phone calls lightly way back then, it had to be something significant and that something was usually bad. Come to think of it, when our kids were growing up, some of the phone calls we received were also pretty bad, so that hasn't changed much.

By the time I was ten or so phone calls were no longer a special occasion. Over the years, the old clunky black phone gave way to small, colorful phones, then the touch phone and then the cell phone. I first really became aware of the cell phone when we visited Scandinavia about eight years ago and, while we were sitting in outdoor cafes, saw that every young person walking down the street was talking into a cell phone, so that it seemed they were all talking to one another, and maybe they were. It didn't take long before the cell phone epidemic spread to this country and now people talk on them 24/7 (when did that phrase start?) and if you can't call someone from the airport, when either getting on or getting off a plane, you are definitely out of it.

Another change came with the age of automation. In the good old days, when you made a phone call to a business or a service you would get an actual human being. Now you get ensnared into an automated system and have to deal with a computer that asks you hundreds of questions before you can get anywhere and you usually end up nowhere. But the company does assure you that your phone call is important to them. I'm convinced that the airlines are down to one live person each when you call to get information and they put every conceivable obstacle in your way of reaching that one person.

Let's come back to that iPhone. The cell phone has already also become a camera and I think some cell phones are also music players. Now the iPhone, as I understand it, will also be a computer, a television set and show movies. Maybe for seniors they'll have one that reminds us when to take our pills and where we parked our cars. In any case, Steve Jobs of Apple, which developed the iPhone, is quoted as saying it's "like having your life in your pocket." I'm not sure that I like that concept; isn't "life" a little more than that? In any case, that's the story of the telephone to date and one can only imagine what other transformations it will have in future years. Maybe it will cook our meals, wash our clothes, pay our bills and drive our cars.

I'd intended to look at some other things that have changed over our lifetimes, but see that I'm running out of space so they'll have to wait for future Observations. Meanwhile, does anyone remember when people wrote letters? To be continued.

March 2007 Observations---on Things GTH

A lady who'd bought my book, "Collected Stories, Volume I," was disappointed that it didn't contain any of my Observations on Life's Little Annoyances (LLA's). For this month, I was going to do an Observations on LLA's, but somehow it came out as an Observations on Things Guaranteed to Happen (GTH's) instead. Maybe it was because I experienced a few GTH's in the last day or two. After that long stretch of nice clear weather, on the one night we were going out the rain started. GTH. When we got back, anxious to change into dry clothes, we discovered one of our cats had spit up. GTH.   Okay, here are some things GTH for the rest of the year. In politics: a prominent politician will be caught doing something bad---stealing money, a sexual indiscretion, a DUI---initially deny it, then blame it on his staff, then say everyone else does it, then confess, take full responsibility (but not the blame) and announce that he (or she) is going into rehab. (Yes, San Francisco Mayor Gavin Newsome has anticipated most of this).

It will come out that one of the presidential hopefuls did something horrible in his (or her) youth. The hopeful will initially deny this, then say it was a youthful indiscretion, that everyone else did it, then announce that he (or she) takes full responsibility but has since been born again so it can't be held against him (or her).

In entertainment: a prominent entertainer will say something inflammatory, or maybe just something politically incorrect, about some group, which will then rise up, demand an apology and threaten a boycott. The entertainer will issue an abject apology and go into rehab.

In television, the new season, for 2006-2007, will see at least a dozen new shows based on this season's hits. So there'll be an "Ugly Amy," an "Ugly Carrie," an "Ugly Dotty," and so on down the line. Also, watch out for "Heroic Housewives," in which a band of suburban housewives suddenly discover they have supernatural powers and unite to fight off a group of aliens plotting to take over the local PTA.

The "reality" shows must continue to get more and more extreme so look for something like "Nabbing Osama." In this show, a diverse group of people will be parachuted to a camp on the Afghanistan/Pakistan border and two teams will compete with each other in locating and capturing Osama Bin Laden.

In sports: a noted sports personality will be arrested for drug possession, illegal gun ownership, spousal abuse, failure to pay child support or some other crime. The sports personality will be put on probation and sentenced to six months of community service. If he has an important game or a playoff series coming up, he'll be given time off so that he can participate. (I wrote this before Ron Artest added still another in the long list of sports personality crimes and misdemeanors---neglecting one's dogs.)

Last year's sports personality was Tiger Woods.

Still in sports, a noted athlete will be accused of taking steroids. He (or she) will deny it, then say the tests were flawed, then say he (or she) never "knowingly" took them.

A former coach-of-the-year will be fired after his team has a losing season. He'll be replaced by another coach with a lifetime losing record. The team will continue losing.

In government: the two political parties will debate some pressing issue. The President will present his plan, but it will be dead on arrival at Congress. After accusations and finger-pointing by both sides, a commission will be appointed to study the issue. After a while, a report will be put out. Nothing will happen.

The so-called health care reform bill? You can name others.

Well, you get the idea; GTH's are a kind of cousin to LLA's. If any of the above has offended anyone, I'll apologize in advance, say it was unintentional and inadvertent, and if necessary go into rehab. Should meet a lot of interesting people in there.

April 2007 Observations---on the Passing Scene

There are always things to marvel at in watching the passing scene on television or reading about it in the newspapers. Here are some recent observations.

Politics, State: our State legislature is back in session and hard at work to solve the problems of California. Among the noteworthy proposed bills, one to jail parents for spanking their kids, and one to hand out $500 for every newborn child. So if the kids misbehave, the parents, instead of spanking them, can fine them up to $500.

I think this bill died a well-deserved death. In any case, in 2010 prisoners are now being released from jail to save money.

By the way, isn't California still a few billion dollars in the red? Nobody except the Legislative Analyst seems to be at all concerned about this.

Let's release those prisoners from jail and balance the budget.

Politics, National--- the next presidential election isn't until November 2008. Do we have to endure daily stories on this for the next two years? Evidently, the answer is, Yes. Are the candidates already attacking each other? Again, the answer is, Yes. By the time the primaries, and then the election, come around it's guaranteed that every candidate will be covered in mud and we'll be left wondering how come all these despicable people aren't in jail. Can't we at least wait until next year before the mud-slinging starts?

Television Cable News: lately, I've been learning all about Anna Nicole Smith. I had no choice because every time I turned on the TV news there was another story about Anna Nicole Smith. Things became so bad that our old friend Britney Spears had to shave her head to even get noticed.

A much more intriguing story to my mind is the tale of the lady astronaut who drove across country, in diapers as the media was always careful to inform us, to attack the woman who had taken her boy friend. The lady astronaut was married, her boy friend was married and the other woman was married. All of them were NASA employees so presumably were intelligent people, not airheads like, say, Britney Spears. So what's going on in our space program? This story seems to have fallen by the wayside. Was it the Anna Nicole Smith effect, or is it a NASA hush-up? I expect to at least see a TV movie about it on Lifetime.

I'm not sure if a movie was made of this. Now the space program, at least going to the moon, has been ended. Any connection? .

Television Shows: the viewing public seems to be at last getting tired of shows which keep posing questions without giving answers while going off in all kinds of directions. After a few seasons, we just don't care that much any more. And it's no longer a big jolt when it's announced that on the next show one of our main characters is going to be killed. Go ahead and kill him (or her), I say; in fact, kill them all off and let's start over with a new show that makes some sense (it's not the Black Donnelys).

Sports: I say, Let's keep Bibby. What's that, Bibby wasn't traded after all, so we still have him. Okay, then let's concentrate on playing basketball. Those other teams in the league aren't that good (Golden State has collapsed) so the Kings can still make the play-offs. (This is written in early March so I hope I won't look too silly by April 1). Then we can resume the discussion about a new arena. Why not build it where everything else is being built, Placer County?

Personal: who cares that much about our politicians, TV or even the Kings? Far more important is that our grandson was born to our son Chris and his wife Flindie in Galway, Ireland. The baby's name is Logan Oliver Green. Our son says the Irish government gives parents 150 Euros a month until age 16 or 18, not a paltry $500. And there's no law about spanking, not that our grandson will ever need it as he'll be the perfect child.

May 2007 Observations

I have fond memories of our short getaway to Maui, especially at this moment when I have a cold and it's raining here in Roseville. Ah, those balmy days and great sunsets.

Observations Goes to Maui

Maybe it's the ocean. Maybe it's the beach. Maybe it's the sound of the ocean waves breaking on the beach. Maybe it's the warm humid air. Maybe it's the tall palm trees swaying in the wind. Maybe it's all of these. Whatever it is, there's something about a tropical vacation, in this case a week in Maui, that drains away all your cares and leaves you relaxed, with perhaps just enough energy left to signal for another Mai Tai or Pina Colada.

My wife Beverly and I had been to Hawaii twice before. The first time, many years ago, we went with our three sons and spent most of our time in Oahu, going to the Polynesian Center, visiting the Pearl Harbor Memorial, joining the crowd on Waikiki Beach, going to a luau, in other words doing all of the typical tourist things. Hardly relaxing. The second time, about three years ago, we went to Maui for the wedding of our son Michael (to Bridget), an exciting time but again not too relaxing.

This spring we decided to return to Maui on our own, to do nothing in particular, and this is pretty much what we did. As we didn't know anything about Maui we chose to stay at the same hotel, the Royal Lahaina, as we did when there for our son's wedding. We discovered that the hotel had been considerably renovated, and also that their prices had considerably risen, since the last time. But we've always found Hawaii to be expensive; it comes with being islands in the middle of the Pacific. I decided to just charge everything to our hotel room so as not to receive a daily shock, saving this for a one-time blow when checking out.

We did find out there was an advantage to being seniors as we were upgraded to a room, on the seventh floor, with a full ocean view. We spent a lot of time just sitting on our little balcony watching the activities on the ocean, sailboats gliding by, and on the beach, kids playing in the surf. And, for the first time in our travels, we actually saw whales. Before this, if there was a whale-sighting on, say, a cruise, we'd always be on the wrong side of the ship. Maui was a big whaling center between 1825 and 1860 and today humpback whales journey from Alaska to Maui to give birth, and I suppose to enjoy the warm waters, from January through March. On our second morning there, we heard about whale-sightings at breakfast and figured that as usual we'd missed them. But then we returned to our room, went out on the balcony and there they were, jumping around in the water. We could finally say we'd seen whales.

We also spent a lot of time in the hotel restaurant, which is an open air place looking west out on the ocean. As the restaurant was open air, we usually had a number of small birds joining us in our meals. It was always pleasant starting the day with a leisurely buffet breakfast. It was also pleasant to have dinner there while watching the sun set. The hotel has a nice custom of having three of their young male employees blowing conch horns to signify the sunset and then lighting torches around the pool while Hawaiian music plays for two young ladies in Hawaiian dress gracefully dancing.

Well, we didn't spend all of our time loafing around (and eating) at the hotel. We roused ourselves enough to take a tram (free) to the nearby Whaler's Village, twice, and the tram and a bus (one dollar each) to Lahaina, three miles away. I'd noticed that all the men in Maui dressed casually and that most wore some kind of necklace. In other places, the necklace-wearing might have seemed odd but in Maui it seemed natural. As soon as we entered Hilo Hattie's in Lahaina a nice Hawaiian young lady placed a shell necklace around my neck so I too joined the crowd. Aside from its restaurants and shops, we discovered that Lahaina has many, many art galleries, a sort of Pacific Carmel, and many of the artists were quite good.

Whalers Village, like Lahaina, has enough shops and restaurants for an afternoon's visit. It also has a Whalers Museum, where I obtained my information about Maui's whaling history. I also learned that while whaling might have been a profitable industry for some, a common seaman made all of about $30 for a four-year voyage. I mentioned that things in Maui were somewhat expensive. In Tommy Bahama's I saw some colorful shirts that looked nice; they were over $100. But admission to the Whalers Museum was free.

Although we didn't do much, time in Maui somehow went by quickly and all too soon our last evening there arrived. We had our last sunset dinner and our last sunset drink. The next day we'd return to Sun City where we had to do something about the ground cover that had been killed by the winter's frost and attend to all those other household matters and then there'd be Iraq and Iran and North Korea and the latest worldwide troubles. But for the time being we'd just watch the sun disappear into the Pacific while the sound of the waves lapping up on the beach lulled us into soft contentment.

June 2007 Observations---on Books Again

Last June, Observations looked at some of the books I (and I'm sure other Sun Cityites) read as kids, and promised "more later." Well, it only took a year, but here is a look at some other books. A year ago, I mentioned Edgar Rice Burroughs, who wrote the Tarzan books. Burroughs is a classic American case of rags-to-riches, a man who was a drifter, had one low-paying job after another, then, after reading the pulp magazines popular at that time and deciding he could do as well, became arguably our most successful writer.

Burroughs first Tarzan book, "Tarzan of the Apes," came out in 1912 so he had plenty of time to enjoy his late-life success. I didn't know that he was living in Hawaii at the time of Pearl Harbor and that he became the oldest war correspondent during World War II. About his being arguably our most successful author, Burroughs created a character known the world over. I don't know if kids still read his books (I hope they do) but probably most have seen the movies based on them on television. What more could you ask?

In all, Burroughs wrote 26 Tarzan books. He also wrote science-fiction books, about people going to Mars and other planets, as well as Westerns and historical novels. Once the man got started, there was evidently no stopping. Last year, I also mentioned H.G. Wells' early science-fiction novels. Wells of course is known for much more than these, having written several acclaimed novels, a history of the world and being a leading British intellectual.

His sci-fi novels created a number of genres that have persisted until today. One was that of Earth being invaded by superior beings from other planets. The first words of "The War of the Worlds" still send a chill through me: "No one would have believed that this world was being watched keenly and closely by intelligences greater than man's …" And then continuing with: "Yet across the gulf of space, minds that are to our minds are to those of the beasts that perish, intellects vast and cool and unsympathetic, regarded the earth with envious eyes, and slowly and surely drew their plans against us."

Wells also wrote "The Time Machine," inspiring countless other books, TV shows and movies to this day. Wells was not too optimistic about the future of our world, although he did not predict its end by global warming (or freezing). He foresaw a society with a rather effete race, the Eloi, who live a life of ease, and the Morlocks, who live underground and provide for the Eloi. (Crossword puzzle fans take note as one or both of these are frequent answers.) The only drawback to being an Eloi is that the Morlocks also eat them. Another Wells' books is "The Invisible Man," another theme which has gotten never-ending use. Probably all of us at one time or another has toyed with the idea of being invisible and what we'd do if we were. Wells' story carries the message that it's not really easy being invisible and his hero comes to a sad end.

I'll mention just one more science-fiction writer, Jules Verne, a Frenchman whose dates are 1828-1905, and whose books also foresaw many inventions which eventually came to pass. "Twenty Thousand Leagues Under the Sea" predicted the submarine, with the Nautalis, commanded by the unforgettable Captain Nemo (crossword fans again take note). "From the Earth to the Moon" pretty well foresees our space program, the space ship being launched from Florida. The 1959 movie based on Verne's book, "Journey to the Center of the Earth," was at one time shown on television just about every week. The cast includes Pat Boone, James Mason, Arlene Dahl, Diane Baker and Gertrude the Duck. Verne also wrote "Around the World in Eighty Days," the basis for the hit movie.

There must be something about science fiction that appeals, not just to kids, but to everyone as shown by the persistence of the themes developed by Burroughs, Wells and Verne in today's movies and television. If most of us have toyed with the idea of being invisible, probably we've also dreamed about venturing into space and thought about going backward and forward in time. I still remember at least parts of the Tarzan and the other books and am reminded of them almost every week when watching TV.

Astute readers may have guessed that I had a reason for once again writing about books and they'd be right. My second book, "Collected Stories, Volume II," is now out. Please see the article elsewhere in this issue telling all about it and how to get it (only $10 this time) and thank you in advance for supporting your local author.

July 2007 Observations

I wonder how many remember the Virginia Tech shootings now, three years later. More recently we've had the Fort Hood shootings and the Christmas bomber, or would-be-bomber. The same observation applies. The privacy of the individual has been given priority over the safety of the community. Political correctness has a lot to answer for.

As Observations readers know, this space is usually reserved for taking a look at the lighter side of things, in Sun City and elsewhere. But sometimes an event occurs that makes it difficult to be light-hearted and prompts more serious thoughts. Although this won't appear until July, it's being written a few weeks after the Virginia Tech murders and that event has raised some troublesome questions, about the event itself and about a number of other things that have come about since the time our generation were kids and the present when we've become senior citizens.

For example, as we've started with Virginia Tech, a college, what's happened to education during our lifetime? When I was a kid, it was taken for granted that we'd go to school and learn our reading, writing and arithmetic as well as other things like history and geography and, as I recall, most of us did just that. I keep hearing on the radio messages that California schools are in desperate shape and need more money. These messages, not surprisingly, are sponsored by the California Teachers Association. Well, we've been hearing this for as long as I can remember and we even have a law mandating that a pretty fair percentage of the state's total budget go to education. And it's still a mess.

Our generation went to school during the Great Depression and its aftermath and I can't believe that our schools way back then had a lot of money. We also hear today about our disadvantaged students. In the 1930's and 1940's, we were all disadvantaged. Not only were we poor, but, as in my case, we were in single-parent families, my father having gone out of town to do "defense work" in 1939. Yet we still managed to get a reasonable education. Not only this, but our schools were safe. Kids back then didn't carry guns and knives as a matter of course. And the teachers' word was law.

We also felt safe walking to and back from school. When I was a kid I wouldn't have known what a "pedophile" was. Where did they all suddenly come from? We also didn't have sexual abuse, something, to judge from their confessions, just about every movie star has suffered from. Just as in the school the teachers' word was law in my family my fathers' word (when he was home) was law. When we did something bad, he even, horrors!, spanked us, although with sorrow and not very hard. Nowadays some of our lawmakers want to make this a felony.

Jumping from school to another important part of our life, entertainment, when we were kids we listened to such radio programs as "Jack Armstrong," "The Lone Ranger," "The Shadow," "Jack Benny" and "Fred Allen." You know what the kids have today, on television, in the movies and on the internet. It's almost mandatory that there has to be obscenity and sex, the more, it seems, the better.

Going back to the Virginia Tech event, here was a guy who did everything but walk around with a sign around his neck saying, "Time Bomb Waiting To Go Off " and nobody did anything about it. How did he even get to be a senior in college? And once he got into Virginia Tech, what does it take to get expelled from college today? Evidently, stalking two coeds on separate occasions and frightening his teachers wasn't enough. I was going to sum up what has happened in our lifetime in a few profound sentences, but I happened to come across an article in the Wall Street Journal (by Daniel Henninger) that does this much better than I ever could. Senator Joseph Lieberman is quoted as saying, "We want to respect the privacy of the individual, yet ultimately I think wa have a greater responsibility to protect the safety of the community.' Henninger comments: "Sound sensible? If embraced by our politics, that notion would overturn 40 years of jurisprudence and conventional wisdom that, of late, has turned deadly."

I would add just one thing, that in addition to the notion that the community's safety has priority, I'd like to see a return to old-fashioned common sense (as opposed, say, to political correctness). Common sense tells us that something should have been done. Let's hope that in the future common sense will prevail.

August 2007 Observations

Ireland was hard hit by the Recession and, like California, has cut back on services and increased taxes. So far our son Chris and his wife Flindie are doing okay and we now have two grandchildren there, Logan, three years old, and Stephanie, going on two. We'll keep visiting them in Ireland as long as we're able to endure the flights over there (and back).

Observations on Ireland

Our third trip to Ireland, last May and June, was a little different from our previous two. Our son Chris and his wife Flindie had a baby, Logan, in February so this time we went, not as tourists, but primarily as grandparents. We stayed in Chris and Flindie's house in Galway our first week there, then moved to an apartment in a Galway suburb, Salthill, for two weeks. In between the times we spent with our new grandson, we did have a chance to see quite a bit of Galway and Salthill so here are the latest Observations on Ireland.

Galway, with a population of a little over 70,000, is the third largest city in Ireland. As our son kept reminding us, Ireland is a small country, about 4 million total population, over half of which is in Dublin. While Dublin is in the East, Galway is on the west coast, situated on the Galway Bay of the song. This being so, Galway is famous for being windy and during our first week there the winds more than lived up to their reputation. Then something strange happened: the winds died down, the sun shone and we had a heat wave, temperatures up in the 70's and even touching 80. So off came the layers of clothing and on came the one pair of shorts I'd luckily packed.

When the sun comes out in Galway, everyone rushes to the Salthill promenade (or Prom), at two miles the longest one in Ireland. When I say "everyone" I mean just that; crowds of young people, mothers and fathers pushing prams (baby carriages), joggers, power walkers, grandmothers and granddads like Beverly and myself. The tradition is to walk the length of the Prom to what's called the "kicking wall," which you then, no surprise, kick. We were unable to find out when this tradition started and even a Google search was futile, but my observation was that most people did kick the wall. Beverly and I, not to be outdone, of course kicked the wall and have the pictures to prove it, although I won't guarantee that we walked the full length of the Prom.

Galway, like Ireland itself, has prospered in recent years (since the European Union) and our visits to "town" showed this. Shops, restaurants and pubs were all crowded. . There's a pedestrian street, which was enlivened by street musicians, chalk artists and other performers. The newly rebuilt town square. Eyre Square, was full of people, as was the green area by the Spanish Arch at the other end of town. Galway has become a high-tech center (Chris works for a high-tech company). It also has a college, the National University of Ireland (NUI) Galway, which gained some notoriety when actor Martin Sheen enrolled there for a semester last year, and where Flindie works part-time. (Flindie met Sheen and says he's even smaller than onscreen.)

Galway has events the year-long: a spring music festival, an air show, a June arts festival and in August the Galway races, also of the song. It has two theaters and a new city museum, just two-months old when we visited, very modern, by the Spanish Arch. It also has Charlie Byrnes book store, where you can find second-hand books, Penguin editions and the like, you can't usually find here. I can't really say too much about the restaurants because Irish cuisine, as far as I could tell, consists of having a lot of potatoes, mashed or fried (chips) with every meal (this may bring the wrath of my in-laws down on me). Galway, being on the Bay, did offer a certain amount of seafood. Fish and chips was always a good bet, as was seafood chowder, especially during that first cold, windy week. .

Something about Salthill. It's a tourist mecca, in Ireland at any rate, and so is filled with hotels and the ubiquitous B&B's. Chris and Flindie found us an apartment, cost less and was much better suited for a two-week stay, having a living room, two bedrooms, a kitchen and a dining area, a dishwasher, a microwave and even a washer-dryer. We had a big book of instructions on how to use everything, plus little notes next to every switch and appliance so even us Americans couldn't go too far wrong. Besides the Prom, where we took our daily stroll, Salthill has restaurants, pubs, markets, a post office, casinos, even a very nice aquarium, and any place selling ice cream has a big cone outside so you can't miss it. As stated above, on a sunny day everyone comes to the Prom and you know those scenes in movies about Ireland with crowded pubs where the TV is blaring out a Gaelic football or some such game and everyone is wearing those colorful rugby shirts; well, that describes the pubs by the Prom at such times.

Although we didn't do too much touring, one place we went to should be mentioned, Lady Gregory's old home by Coole Lake, which is very close to Galway. Lady Gregory was a co-founder of Ireland's famous Abbey Theater and her home was a literary center. Although the home is now gone, the grounds have a deer park, nice gardens and walks and the "autograph tree," on which are inscribed the names of William Butler Yeats, George Bernard Shaw, Sean O'Casey and John Synge, among others. I said Ireland was a small island; while there we met a couple who'd been at Chris and Flindie's wedding, also pushing a pram and now living in Limerick.

One last observation: the Irish people are the friendliest we've met overseas, even more so than the French (that's a joke). The people say "hello," drivers give you the right-of-way, you can sit outside a pub with a Guinness or Irish coffee and never be rushed. Several times, when we were ready to leave, we were just asked what we'd had and never questioned. Altogether, a relaxed syle of life.

Well, we had, as they say, a "grand time" during our Irish stay. Now that we're back, we're trying to get used to saying diapers instead of nappies, parking lots instead of car parks and closets instead of presses. A PS:: the response to the announcement of my new book. "Collected Stories, Volume II," in June's issue was pretty underwhelming, so a reminder, it can be had for a mere $10. Send a check (or cash) to 7604 Timberrose Way and I'll be happy to deliver. It's truly a "grand' book.

September 2007 Observations

I believe I've mentioned in this space before that going on a bus tour is not a vacation. I'm reminded of this observation by the recent bus tour Beverly and I took through the Canadian Rockies. As most readers know, it's a cardinal rule of such tours that no matter what the day's activities are they start early in the morning, preferably at eight and certainly no later than nine. In fact, any respectable tour director who allows his charges to start the day's tour at nine will be charged with coddling them. And on those days when the tour bus is going from one stop to the next it's usually bags out at 6:30, bus leaves at 7:30. This is even though nothing in particular is scheduled when you reach your destination.

Another cardinal rule of bus tours is to have mornings or afternoons or sometimes even whole days "at leisure." What this means is that the tour company washes its hands of you for those times and you are on your own in a strange city wondering what to do. One of the things you want to do of course is to find a place to eat. You've asked your tour director, but, like a good director, he doesn't want to coddle those senior citizens, so he (or she) has given you some vague response, like, oh, go down that street and you'll find plenty of places. Yeah, right. You also get a map at your hotel desk and ask there about places to eat. The response is usually the same as the tour director's. If the desk person does give you the name of some restaurant and tells you that it's only a five minute walk it's almost certain to be 20 or 30 minutes away and the weather at these times is always hot so that you're tired and sweating by the time you find the place, if you do.

Did I mention that on bus tours the weather is almost never what you'd expected it to be. Going on this Canadian Rockies tour, we expected it to be fairly cool. After all, you're up there in the mountains, like at Lake Tahoe. But for some reason, maybe global warming, for this tour it was unseasonably hot. So we never got to wear the sweaters and jackets we packed and I'm glad I threw in that one pair of shorts. Another thing that almost always happens on a bus tour is that one of the hotels selected by the tour company is terrible. On this tour, it was our first hotel, where our room was tiny, the closet door was broken, the air conditioner was loud and when we asked for a wake-up call at 7:10 (early enough) we got one at 6:30. Other passengers reported that their air conditioners leaked or didn't work at all. And, almost guaranteed to happen, with the unseasonably hot weather, one of our hotels didn't even have air-conditioning. It had never been that hot there before.

Another thing that happens on all bus tours is that the passengers play games of one-upmanship. One game is to have gone on more tours and to have been to more places than any of the other tourists. If you mention that you've recently been to Ireland, which we had, to visit our son, you'll immediately be informed that they've been to Ireland, Scotland, England, Wales, India, China and the North Pole. Another game of one-upmanship is to tell the other passengers what great places they've found and great things they've done on those "at leisure" times. So, you'll be told, We met this couple and they invited us to their home, we had a fabulous dinner, and they turned out to be the Mayor and his wife. .

Nevertheless, at the end of every bus tour, there is the "farewell dinner," at which everyone tells each other what a great trip, no matter how arduous, it was, how great the tour director (even if he barely noticed you) was and how wonderful all the passengers were. As you get up to leave, fellow tourists who hadn't spoken a word to you all during the trip come up, gush about how nice it was to meet you, shake hands, hug you, and are distraught because it's all over and they'll never see you again.

Reading through the above, maybe I've exaggerated a little and I should mention that bus tours have their plus sides. Your suitcases are taken care of, you get a lot of information about the places you visit that you wouldn't get if on your own, your tour group gets in some places ahead of ordinary tourists, many of your meals are provided and most are pretty good. And, on this Canadian Rockies trip, we got to see some spectacular scenery, had a few days in Vancouver, an interesting city, had lunch at beautiful Lake Louise and now know what Jasper and Bampff are like. We also saw a few mountain sheep, a half dozen elk and two black bears. So, after we've recovered, we'll probably be looking into bus tours again. But not for a while.

October 2007 Observations

The TV show "Mad Men," the subject of the "Observations" below, has in its three seasons become a big hit. I'm still following the ups and downs in the career of the hero, Don Draper. It seems that the woman in the show, including Don's long-suffering wife, have become more self-assertive as it's gone on. Don, and other characters, are still puffing away at those cigarettes. I assume that sooner or later they all succumbed to lung cancer.

One of the better things on television this summer, despite its title, was a show called "Mad Men." The show was set in New York City in the 1950's and was about advertising, the "Mad Men" referring, not to a bunch of lunatics, but men who worked on Madison Avenue, where most of the leading ad agencies were located. The first episode was mainly concerned with a campaign for Lucky Strikes cigarettes when, even way back then, the tobacco industry was beginning to come under attack.

The show held special interest for me because when I returned to New York City from the Army in the 1950's my first job interview was with an advertising agency and the first questions were about how best to market cigarettes. I don't remember exactly what my answers were, maybe to have people hand out free samples, because that's what they'd done in the Army. So I might be responsible for all of those young ladies who used to go out on the streets giving innocent bystanders free cigarettes. No, I think they were already doing this. At any rate, whatever my answers, I got the job.

The most distinctive thing about the show "Mad Men" is that everyone in it smokes constantly so that all of the action takes place in clouds of smoke. You have to believe that everyone who worked on Madison Avenue in the 1950's died young of lung cancer. Although some people in my ad agency smoked, if it was as bad as the show depicts I'm sure I would have been coughing all the time. I had smoked for a while in the Army but not afterwards, possibly because I no longer got free samples.

Cigarettes are of course now virtually outlawed and it won't be long that in California anyone lighting up will be shot on sight. A number of other things pop up in "Mad Men," that no longer exist today. The men all wear white shirts, ties of course, and hats. I recall wearing white shirts and ties but never wore a hat, which might explain why I never rose very high in the ad game. The secretaries use a machine called a typewriter. Remember them? When I went off to college I found out that you couldn't write papers by hand any more and so my parents got me a second-hand typewriter. I wonder where that went. I'm reminded that back in those days people used to write with fountain pens and that a common high school graduation present was a fancy pen and pencil set.

"Mad Men" reminded me that in the 1950's there were elevator operators, who somehow seemed necessary to make elevators go up and down. When I came to Sacramento in the 1960's there were still elevator operators in the Capitol building, probably the last of the species. Another vanished occupation is "telephone operator," those women who made the old telephone system work. I was trying to think of other occupations that have disappeared and came up with those men who used to deliver coal and ice, the vegetable man who used to bring around fresh vegetables on his horse and cart, the milk man, the insurance man who used to come around to collect his few pennies (or dollars) every week and who was virtually a part of the family, and maybe hat-makers (there can't still be many of those around.)

Yes, it was a different world in the 1950's. Another thing I recall is that my starting salary at the ad agency was a big $60 a week. No wonder I didn't buy a hat. A major theme running through "Mad Men" is that the women ("girls" back then) who worked in those ad agencies were, shall we say, very accommodating to the men. I don't remember this being true in my case. If I'd been able to light a cigarette with that certain flair, and look terribly sophisticated while exhaling the smoke through my nostrils I might have done better. Still, I look back with some fondness on being a small part in what was then considered a glamorous industry. After a short time, I left all that glamour, my paycheck increased to more than $60 a week but I still didn't buy a hat.

November 2007 Observations

What, it's November already. The year has almost gone by and not, as far as I can recall, a single Observations on Life's Little Annoyances (LLA's). Next month is December, Christmas, peace and good will and all that, so before it's too late an LLA update.

Where to begin? The daily mail is always good for some LLA's. First, there's the delivery itself. Our mail usually comes in the early afternoon, but every so often it doesn't come until late or even late, late afternoon, so there you are, trekking out to the mailbox three of four times before the mail is there. Annoying. But not as annoying as what comes in the mail---junk, bills and more junk. Most annoying to me are the solicitations from all those credit card companies. They're never satisfied with your signing up for a credit card; they keep sending you things urging you to sign up for even more expensive credit cards. And they keep coming in a steady stream, as relentless as Democrat attacks on President Bush or Republican attacks on Hillary Clinton.

The above comparison was a way to segue to another LLA, the all-year-round and seemingly endless campaigning for president. Given the kind of campaigns we've had in recent years---smear, smear, smear---by November of next year, when the elections will finally occur, we'll be wondering how any of the candidates have managed to stay out of jail. Or maybe, by that time, we'll all have tuned out.

This brings us to another one of life's little annoyances (maybe one of life's greatest annoyances if you pay any attention to it), the modern media. Enough has been said about this by others so I needn't belabor the point here. I'll just say: Princess Diana, Anna Nicole Smith, Britney Spears. O.J. Simpson, Michael Vick, Don Imus, Al Sharpton, and on and on. Enough already.

It goes without saying that television commercials are by their very existence a source of annoyance. But I'd like to comment on my pet peeve, those commercials featuring little kids talking like grownups, usually about stocks, bonds, mutual foods, healthy foods, and usually admonishing foolish adults to buy these products. No, I don't think these TV kids are cute and I'm not likely to buy a mutual fund because some kid sounding like a chipmunk tells me to. .

Going to print media, the Sacramento Bee can always be depended on for some LLA's. As the paper itself has told us, it's trying to cut costs and is therefore downsizing. Unfortunately, the TV guide has been downsized so much that it's become almost useless and the Forum has become much less interesting. And, really annoying and having nothing to do with cutting costs, the Bee persists in having both Sunday crossword puzzles on the same double page so that they have to be either cut or torn apart. With everything else, is this necessary? Or should we be thankful that the crossword puzzles haven't been downsized, too? Another little annoyance is that the Bee is the only newspaper in town.

I've saved the worst LLA for last and that of course is going to the airport. As with our media, many other people have written about today's airport experience, one likening it to a trip to hell. I'm annoyed primarily because after all this time I'd hoped that some common sense would be applied to security checks. But no, every senior citizen, wheel chair occupant, nun and kindergarten kid is still being scrutinized. On our last trip, a pair of my nail scissors I'd forgotten I'd left in Beverly's carry-on was confiscated, as she told me while I was putting my shoes back on. Why doesn't this make me feel any better about our nation's security?

Okay, these are the LLA"s for this year. As stated above, December is the time for peace and good will. Maybe we'll take a look at the events of the year 2007---Princess Di, Anna Nicole Smith, Britney Spears, O.J. Smith, Michael Vick, Don Imus, Al Sharpton … Oh, no. There must be something else. That's enough for now.

December 2007 Observations

Some months ago in this space I predicted that, as last season's big hit TV show was "Heroes," this season would feature shows like "Heroic Housewives." The TV listings don't include "Heroic Housewives," but there's almost every other variation on the "Heroes" theme. For those few readers who have never heard of "Heroes," this is a show featuring what we may call "people of special abilities," a more accurate description than "Heroes" as some are not necessarily heroic and a few are downright villainous. There's a politician who can not only lie with a straight face but can fly, a teenage cheerleader whose body can heal itself of any injury, an artist who can paint pictures foretelling the future, a Japanese fellow who can transport himself back and forth in time, you get the idea. The plot lines of the show, and they are many, are pretty murky; some of the characters want to kill some of the others, and there was something about averting a nuking of New York (which some might think a good idea).

Anyway, in the wake of "Heroes" tremendous popularity, we now have shows starring a guy who can bring people back from the dead with a touch of his finger, but another touch and they're dead again; a guy who goes back in time. yes, like the Japanese guy (and Scott Baluka) but he has no control over when this happens; a nerd whose mind got crammed full of top-secret information; another nerd whose parents sold his soul to the Devil and now he must--- well, I think that's enough; but I mustn't forget that, thanks to "Heroes," the Bionic Woman is back. Wonder if "Wonder Woman" can be far behind?

So, what does this all mean? Yes, to us keen social observers, it must mean something, not just that the TV people hope there's a big audience out there for dumb, comic-book style shows. Well, let's see, the country is stuck in an unpopular war and nobody seems to be able to do much about it. Then there's the collapse of the housing market with the stock market going all over the place. Then there's global warming and the imminent destruction of the world unless we all replace out light bulbs; or, maybe the end is not really imminent but we still have Al Gore out there and that might be even worse. Okay, things are happening that we, ordinary mortals that we are, can't control and in many cases are sick and tired of hearing about. So what does Gotham City do when crime gets out of control? Right, they call for Batman. What do we need? Heroes, that's what, to get things under control.

This brings us to---next year's election. Yes, although nobody except those cable channel talking heads are taking any notice, those debates you may have vaguely heard about are leading to primaries and then to an election in 2008. And who will people want to elect? Naturally, someone who has special abilities, a super-duper-hero. What special abilities did the candidates in the last presidential election have? Bush had a special ability to mangle the English language. Kerry had a special ability to sound like a scold.

What special abilities have the current candidates, whoever they are, shown so far? Let's see, Hillary Clinton is running. She seems to have a special ability to dodge questions, or to take both sides of an issue. Of course, that's true of all politicians, it's the first thing they learn in Politics 1A. Barak Obama? He seems to have the special ability to seem like a nice guy. Uh, oh, that may disqualify him right there. Rudy Giuliani? He has the special ability to bring up 9/11 no matter what's being talked about; and in a New York accent. Mitt Romney? He's a Republican who got himself elected governor of Massachusetts. McCain? You know, this guy might be a genuine hero; and he sometimes speaks his mind, too. No wonder he's so far down in the polls.

Well, as far as I can see, this deep analysis didn't help at all. The truth is that none of our presidential aspirants is a super-hero (not even Hillary looks like a Wonder Woman). Maybe this is not such a bad thing. In the real world, problems aren't usually solved by people who can fly or who can go back and forth in time. Let's just hope that whoever becomes our next President has the ability to see the real world as it is. And in due time I'm sure the craze for people with special abilities will pass and we'll have some other trend on TV. Let's see, what about a plane crashing on a mysterious island; wait, that's been done before. What about ordinary people facing ordinary problems? No, that's too radical an idea. We'll have to wait and see. One more thing: my son Chris has created a web page for me. Anyone wanting to take a look, go to martingreenbook.com.

2008 OBSERVATIONS

January 2008 Observations

Another "Observations" on the coming year, 2008. Maybe I wasn't gloomy enough as the recession did start later that year and this year, 2010, certainly doesn't look too rosy. The partisanship I noted is still evident today and looks as if it will continue into the future. But we didn't completely collapse, as some thought we would, so maybe we'll stagger through once again.

Observations on the Year Ahead

Entering the new year it's easy to feel a little gloomy. The sub-prime mortgage blow-up has shaken up our economy, not to mention decreasing the value of our homes. Economists are talking about a possible recession. Gas prices are over $3 a gallon. The price of a barrel of oil might go over $100. We're still in Iraq. The Iranians may or may not be after nuclear weapons, but in any case they don't like us. Osama keeps threatening us. Then there's the obesity epidemic, bird flu, poisoned toys from China and of course global warming. On top of all this, movies and television are getting even worse. The 49ers and Raiders again had losing years. The Kings are without Kevin Martin and Mike Bibby. Maybe the worst thing in prospect is a presidential election this year. How bad can things get?

I recently listened to a CD my sons had given me containing the 1932 inaugural address of Franklin D. Roosevelt, the one in which he famously said "The only thing we have to fear is fear itself,". and I was reminded of how bad things can really get. A little research on the Great

Depression, popularly designated as starting with the stock market crash of 1929, the year in which I was born (just a coincidence), found that by 1933 almost 13 million people had lost their jobs, the unemployment rate was about 25% and almost $2 billion in bank deposits had been lost. Those were really tough times. Add to this the rise of Hitler in Germany and the threat of Japan in the Pacific.

As a Depression kid, I didn't realize how bad things were, but I do remember that we lived in a Bronx tenement (more than one, actually) where my mother put out potatoes covered with some kind of poison to kill the roaches; my father, a plumber, did jobs for our landlord to pay the rent; he eventually got a job on the WPA and then, starting in 1939, he had to go out of town to find work in what were then known as defense jobs. I wouldn't be surprised if there were times when it was touch and go if we'd have food on our plates that night.

So what do we have today? I know that in our country we still have people who are unemployed, who are hungry and who are homeless. But when I look around I see unbelievable prosperity. I don't know what percentage of our population owns homes, but, despite the recent sub-prime interest crash, I'm sure it's at or close to an all-time high. It seems that almost everyone has a car and many, like those of us in Sun City, have two or three cars, not to mention golf carts. As mentioned above, when I was a kid we lived in a tenement; nobody in our family or that we knew had his own house and nobody had a car.

What's our unemployment rate today? Under five percent. And we have unemployment insurance, social security, Medicare and MediCal, food stamps and I don't know how many other social welfare programs. Did people unwisely take out loans on houses they couldn't afford? The government is trying to fix that, too. And we're awash in cars costing as much as houses once did, plasma TV's, iPods, iMacs, PC's, DVD's, game boxes, cell phones, the list is endless.

Overseas, we have Iraq, Afghanistan, Iran, North Korea and others to contend with. But does any of them compare to Hitler's Germany or Japan at a time when we had virtually no armed forces and were woefully unprepared for any sort of conflict? At least now we have more than enough firepower, although we don't always know when or where to use it.

All in all, things could be worse, a lot worse, as they were in the 1930's. We managed to get through the Great Depression and World War II after that. The one thing that concerns me is the quality of our potential leaders today and the partisanship that has seemingly paralyzed any effective dealing with real problems, such as FDR dealt with starting in 1932. But back then his enemies said Roosevelt was a dilettante and Truman was a small-town political type so maybe we'll be surprised. And FDR was right. Let's go into 2008 being hopeful and not fearful.

February 2008 Observations

The things described in the next "Observations"---dealing with credit cards, magazine subscriptions, letters and calls asking for donations---are still going on today and I still think I should have more free time as a retiree, but something always keeps coming up.

I was a little worried when I retired about what I'd do with all the extra time I'd have once I no longer had to go to an office, eight hours every weekday plus a couple of hours commuting. As it turned out, I needn't have been concerned; outside forces were waiting to step in and keep me busy. First, there were the matters of trusts and long-term care. Every retiree had to have these, according to all the letters, brochures and phone calls that started to bombard us. If we didn't have a trust our money would be tied up for years. If we didn't have long-term care…well, look at those nursing home rates, high enough to bankrupt anyone except Bill Gates and getting higher.

Once these matters were duly considered and resolved, there came the onslaught from the credit card companies. The ordinary credit cards we had weren't good enough. We had to upgrade to silver, then gold, platinum, uranium, whatever the next highest was. If we didn't want to upgrade we had to dispose of all the applications and pseudo-credit cards sent us so that someone else wouldn't get hold of them and appropriate our identities. Then there was the complication of airline miles. What credit cards were best for what airlines? And how soon did we have to use the miles? And suppose the airlines, all going under, should cancel the miles? Question after question. Decision after decision.

Second to the credit cards were the magazine subscriptions. Now that I was retired and had time to read more it seemed that every magazine in the world wanted me to subscribe to it. They were all prepared to give me steep discounts, because I was a senior citizen, because I was a professional, because I was alive, just for the favor of reading them. This was the easy part. The hard part came when I didn't renew a subscription. I learned that no magazine will acknowledge that anyone wishes to do this. They would keep sending the magazine, plus requests (really demands) that you re-subscribe week after week and month after month. Not only this but some magazines would send books I'd supposedly requested. This led to correspondence and phone calls, and still the magazines and calls to re-subscribe keep coming.

It soon appeared that I was not only on every magazine's list but also on the list of every travel company in the world. Almost every day the mail would be filled with brochures and books, many of them big and glossy, which must been terribly expensive to produce, telling of trips we just couldn't not take. And if we'd sign up before a certain date we'd get this incredible discount. I could have spent all my time going through all of this travel literature, evaluating the many different offers. More decisions.

Needless to say, I was also soon on the list of every charity in the world. One donation was enough to bring a weekly solicitation from every one. At first, the charities just sent mailing labels, then they progressed to notepads, wrapping paper, stuffed animals and calendars. And now the calendars start coming in June or July. I don't want to sound mean-spirited and I do donate but I sometimes wonder about all the money spent on solicitation material and think there must be a better way, such as sending one at the beginning of every year and asking if any more should be sent until the next year. As it is, the charity letters have to be combed through every day, after the credit card, magazine and travel company mailings are taken care of.

I've saved the thing that perhaps takes up most of my time and that of course is the computer. This deserves an Observations by itself so I'll just mention here that the computer must be checked several times daily to see if any important e-mails have come and to delete all of the spam e-mails. Uh, oh, I think the mail has just come so I'll have to go out and see what I have to deal with today, after a quick check of my e-mail first.

March 2008 Observations

Another "Observations" on TGH's. I see I noted the New York Giants upset victory in the 2008 Super Bowl. Of course in 2009 the Giants collapsed. Maybe that was a GTH.

What, the March issue is coming up already? Time to have a column on things GTH (Guaranteed to Happen) or else I might forget about it until it's too late. Yes, this is a GTH. I'm writing on the day before the Super Tuesday primaries, so let's start with a few political

GTH's. Each candidate begins by vowing to run a clean, high-minded campaign; at the first sign that he (or she) might be losing it's forget about being high-minded, let's smear that dirty no-good other guy. A GTH, especially if your name is Clinton. Speaking of Clinton, Bill will inject himself into the fray in the most personal way. He just can't help himself. GTH. The polls for one primary or another will turn out to be completely wrong. All of the pundits will sneer at the pollsters, but when the next primary comes around they'll still cite the poll numbers. GTH.

Looking at California's politics, the state will have a budget deficit. GTH. Wasn't Governor Arnold elected because he said he'd do something about this? And now it's bigger than ever. GTH. The Governor will call the Legislature into special session to solve the budget crisis. Nothing will be done. GTH. The Governor will announce a ten percent cut across the board. When I worked for the State this was announced every few years Did it ever work? No. Will it accomplish anything this time. No. GTH, or maybe this is a Guaranteed Not to Happen.

All right, having disposed of the political stuff, let's look at ordinary life GTH's. There's the weather. A short time ago, I had to drive to downtown Sacramento. I hate driving in the rain, especially on freeways, when, if it's raining, drivers will keep going at their normal (too fast) speeds, a GTH, and there'll be accidents, another GTH. So, the day before I had to drive was clear and sunny. So was the day after. The day in between, when I was driving, was raining. A GTH. It's like when I play Keno or Bingo, if I need one number to win all the numbers all around it will come up but never the one needed. A GTH.

In writing here about LLA's (Life's Little Annoyances), I've noted the magazines that, long after you've stopped subscribing to them, keep on sending you books you never ordered. This is not only a LLA but also almost a GTH. The magazine I had in mind, to name names, is Sports Illustrated, which about eight months ago sent me a book I didn't order. I called their Customer Service and actually got to a real person (not a GTH), who told me I could keep the book, but I sent it back anyway. Well, just recently, SI sent me another unordered book. Again, I called Customer Service and again I was told I could keep the book; this time I did. Yes, you already know what happened next. A month or so later came the bill. Definitely a GTH.

As I write this, one of our cats is on the floor by my chair. This is okay. When I'm in my chair reading or watching television, one or the other of our cats is usually nearby. This too is okay. But when at the end of the month I get out my pen, checks and checkbook to pay the bills---well, all cat owners know what happens next. Before I have a chance to settle in my chair, a cat jumps in my lap, knocks the pen out of my hand, disturbs the checks and sits on the checkbook. A cat GTH.

As a long-time (and long-suffering) New York Giants fan, I have to mention the Super Bowl, on the Sunday before Super Tuesday. Of course, the Giants upset win was a GTH. No, not really; it was more of a miracle. But sometimes miracles do happen; let's call that a GTH. Finally, it's now the day after Super Tuesday and all of the candidates are declaring victory of one kind or another. That was easy to predict, a slamdunk GTH.

April 2008 Observations

I still thing the trick for a successful retirement is to find a balance between having too little and too much to do. And I still think retirees shouldn't do things they don't really want to do. When you're a senior citizen, life is too short.

Observations on Things Learned in Retirement

As all faithful Observations readers know---okay, maybe two or three---I not only write this and the Favorite Restaurants column for the Sun Senior News, I also write short stories and have self-published two collections in the last two years. I should mention that a third collection will come out later this year. But this is not about my short story collections, although it would make me happy if more readers would buy them. After so many short stories, I thought I'd try my hand at a longer piece and this has turned out to be a kind of fictionalized memoir I call, "A Year in Retirement." In this, I try to put the things I've learned, or think I've learned, about being retired. I thought I'd share a few of these in Observations, so here goes.

Like many, if not most new retirees, I think I had a secret dread of not being able to fill up the time I'd previously spent working. This led to my taking on a lot of stuff: I enrolled in a class at our community college; I went down to the Sacramento Volunteer Center and wound up being a volunteer there; I tried some other volunteer activities; and then of course I started writing articles, at that time for a weekly alternative newspaper, the Suttertown News; and after this, I volunteered to work one morning a week at the Suttettown News office, editing copy. All of this was in addition to doing what I now had time to do once retired, play a lot of tennis. What I quickly learned is that it's all to easy to overload yourself when you retire and that you should take things slow and easy. In my case, it took me about a year to pare down my activities to those I really wanted to do.

Notwithstanding this caution, I believe it's important in retirement to have some activity or occupation to center your life around in place of your work. I was lucky in that my occupation, which is writing, found me. I was put in touch with the editor of the Suttertown News by one of Beverly's friends. Then Beverly called my attention to a Sacramento Bee Neighbors feature, "My Story." Readers sent in stories of interesting or amusing incidents in their lives; those that were printed got a princely $25. I sent a story in; it was accepted; I had to call Neighbors to give them my social security number and other information; I asked if they took articles from free-lancers. They did and, better yet, they paid $50 for them (the Suttertown News paid nothing). This led me to writing about 150 pieces over the years for Neighbors; and, as you know, I now write for the Sun Senior News.

Another thing I learned over time was that, as a retiree, I didn't have to do things I didn't want to do; well, not all things anyway. As everyone knows, when you work you have to do many things you don't care to, such as getting up at 6:15 in the morning, commuting to an office, attend pointless meetings, send (and receive) numerous memos, contend with stupid bosses, and all the other stuff that goes along with working for a living. As a retiree, I sleep as late as I can whenever I can and I don't go to meetings. I said that I enrolled in a community college class. I discovered that I didn't really like sitting in a classroom (I'd had enough of that); I stuck out that class, but that was it. I also said that I volunteered to do editing one morning a week at the Suttertown News. After a while, I found I didn't like having a commitment to go downtown one morning a week and editing wasn't that much fun, so I politely said I was too busy with other things to continue doing this.

Still, I think it's beneficial to do something with other people, to replace the things you used to do with your fellow workers. This is the great advantage of living in a place like Sun City. There are numerous clubs you can join to get together with people who have common interests. There are also committees you can serve on to exercise your skills, or maybe develop new skills, and at the same time contribute to your community.

May 2008 Observations

It was tough doing without a microwave, even for a few days. A cell phone I can do without, therefore giving away my advanced age, but the TV and my computer, I don't think so.

Observations on Things We Cannot do Without

Not long ago we had a major disaster in our household; our microwave went out. We reacted in the only sensible way possible---PANIC! How did we heat up coffee before? How could we boil water? How could we heat up leftovers? How could I make my grilled ham sandwiches? We roughed it for almost a full week before finally a new microwave was put in. It was a grim time.

The breakdown of our microwave brought up the question: what other things in our house couldn't we do without if they stopped working, disintegrated or exploded? The most obvious other appliance was also in the kitchen, the dishwasher. Wasn't there a time way back when that people washed, and dried, dishes by hand? I seem to recall that there was something called "dishpan hands" and that there something which was supposed to miraculously cure this.

Then there are the washer and dryer. I remember that as a kid we had a washboard in our house (apartment, really) and that my mother used this to wash clothes. I also remember my father sitting on the window sill as he hung out clothes on a line stretching from our building to the one opposite. I was always afraid he'd fall out, but he never did. I know I wouldn't like to try doing this. When we were in Ireland a couple of years ago we learned firsthand that not everyone in the world has a washer and dryer. Our son Chris and our daughter-in-law Flindie did have a washing machine in the house they were renting but no dryer. Because electricity cost so much, dryers were rare. Instead, as Flindie said, you waited until the sun came out, also pretty rare, then rushed to hang out your clothes on the line in the back yard. I have a picture of Beverly actually doing this.

If our television went out we'd be able to survive, but what would life be without all those great programs (ha, ha) to watch. Would we be reduced to reading books? Playing games? Doing needlepoint? Maybe even talking to each other? It's a frightening prospect. And what about that indispensable instrument, the remote? It's hard to recall, but there was a time when we actually had to get up out of our chairs and walk all the way over to the TV set when we wanted to turn it on or off. How did we ever manage to do this? If the remote went out, would we be able to do this again? Of course not.

Another indispensable device, at least to the younger generation, is the cell phone, also used to watch television, listen to music, connect with the internet, change lead to gold; well, maybe it can't do the last. Beverly and I have cell phones, but I guess we're too old-fashioned to use them as a matter of course. But I know that without cell phones, half of our television shows couldn't be written as they are. What would Jack Bauer do if he couldn't call the President with his trusty cell phone or if Chloe couldn't call him with her cell phone? He couldn't function. and Los Angeles would by now have been blown to bits several times over.

Then there's the device I'm using to write this column on, the PC, or personal computer. How did people communicate with each other before they had their PC's? When we first moved to Sun City, people actually phoned each other to set up committee or club meetings. Now it's all done by e-mail. And if someone doesn't have a PC (I know this is unthinkable), then what? I really don't know. Maybe they'd have to resort to the phone, or carrier pigeon, or something. I seem to recall a time when people wrote each other letters. This is now a practice as quaint as washing and drying dishes or washing clothes by hand.

Our new microwave has been installed and is working. What about the future? I'm sure there'll come a day when, as I used to see on Star Trek, you'll put a couple of tablets on a tray, insert into the microwave (of the future) and out will come a steak dinner with strawberry shortcake as a dessert. Meanwhile, we hope for no more breakdowns in the near future. We need some time to recover from having to struggle along without a microwave all that time.

June 2008 Observations

It's always interesting going to Las Vegas because Las Vegas is always changing. The big casino/hotels seem close to one another, but it takes hours to walk to them, even to the casino next door. I see I didn't mention seeing Pete Rose (the baseball player) on this trip. He was busy signing things in a bookstore as we walked by, was wearing a baseball cap and looked like, who else, Pete Rose.

Observations Goes to Las Vegas

Every spring Beverly and I like to take a little getaway from our arduous Sun City retirement life. This year we decided to try that getaway place of all getaways, Las Vegas. One of the hotels offered in our Expedia package was Caesar's Palace. We'd never stayed there and, apart from going through its Forum shops, had never really explored Caesar's, so that seemed a good place to choose.

We knew Caesar's was large but never realized how vast it was, just a little bit smaller than the original Roman Empire, until we spent a few days there. There's the hotel with half a dozen or so different "towers," two casinos, the Forum shops area, which is boundless, and innumerable corridors and spaces. Fortunately, Caesar's provides its guests with a map or we'd never have found our way through it.

We expected that the buffet, in keeping with the rest of Caesar's, would be large and sumptuous. Surprisingly, it was the smallest of the hotel/casino buffets we've yet eaten at. However, everything there was of good quality and there was more than enough to satisfy our appetites. You also looked out on the pool area, which is built to resemble a Roman bath, so you could imagine you were dining in Rome. We started our days by having breakfast there. As soon as we were seated at a table, orange juice and coffee were brought. At the buffet, eggs were cooked to your order. The other usual breakfast items---fruit, pancakes, waffles, ham, bacon, sausages and all kinds of pastries--- were all there for the taking. It was nice to linger over our coffee, knowing that our room was being made up, and making plans for another self-indulgent day.

In the spirit of self-indulgence, I went to Caesar's spa, called the Qua, on our second afternoon there. In order to tire myself out before going there to relax, I walked across the street (or Strip) to the Tropicana. This involved going over two bridges and going up and down escalators and took about half an hour. I then walked around the gardens in back of the Tropicana, which were very nice, looking for the flamingo exhibit that was supposed to be there. I finally located it, but, as often seems to happen to "free" attractions in Las Vegas, it was closed. So I walked back, another half an hour, and by this time was more than ready for the Qua.

You can spend hundreds of dollars in the Qua if you want individual massages, etc., but I chose the basic package for a mere $45. As soon as I checked in (and paid), I was handed a white robe and blue plastic sandals. My guide showed me the lockers, where I stored my clothes, offered me orange juice, which I took and carried with me, and showed me the different parts of the Qua. I started with the Roman bath, a large hot tub, where I sat for a while, listening to soothing music, then dried off on a lounge chair. I should mention that the Qua is separated by sexes so no maidens fanned me or offered me drinks, but I still had my orange juice.

After this, I went to another bath, then tried the eucalyptus room, a kind of sauna, then cooled off by going into the "Ice Room," where the temperature is 54 degrees and icicles come down from the ceiling. Then it was time to go into the "Tea Room," where guys in white robes relaxed in armchairs with foot rests while sipping drinks and eating fruit or pretzels. And, oh, yes, there was a TV with sports (this was a guys' thing) on it. Altogether, I spent about two hours in the Qua, and returned to our room, where Beverly was relaxing with a book, ready for the evening dinner buffet.

As we'd gone to the Caesar's buffet the night before and that morning, we decided we'd have enough of Rome and so went across the street, another half-hour trek, to the Paris for dinner. The Paris buffet has a good reputation and there was a long waiting line, but it moved fairly quickly and we passed the time by talking with our fellow waiters, who were from England. I noticed a lot of English accents at Las Vegas, also French and German, and surmised that people were coming over here to take advantage of changing their Euros or pounds for twice the amount of our weak dollars.

The Paris buffet lived up to its reputation, with food from different parts of France. The feature item, I thought, was the crepes from Brittany, out of this world. We then wandered through the Paris. Whoever designed the hotel/casino did an excellent job as you really felt you were walking through Paris streets, with their cafes and shops, under a Paris sky. But the Paris slot machines weren't as friendly, so it was back to Caesar's.

The next morning we went, not across the Strip this time, but next door to visit Caesar's neighbor, the Bellagio. The way to the Bellagio was through a corridor lined with all of the world's expensive, make that very expensive, shops---Gucci, Prado, Tiffany, I can't remember the rest. The Bellagio itself somehow reeked of money. It was while walking down one of its expansive halls that the thought came: if the money spent on all of these hotel/casinos had been put to some other use, say, alleviating world hunger, it would have, as Beverly said, if not solved the problem, put a big dent in it. The thought that naturally followed was: if we were in a recession you couldn't prove it in Las Vegas.

The flight from Sacramento to Las Vegas is less than two hours, one of the reasons we'd decided to go there. As everyone knows, air travel is one of the worst things you can subject yourself to nowadays, so we wanted to keep it short. Our trip was the week after the American Airlines disaster. I half-expected that our airline, not American, would ground all of its planes for inspection or declare bankruptcy the day we left. However, all went smoothly; we arrived on schedule and our luggage wasn't lost. Still, on returning at the Las Vegas airport, our two carry-ons, which had passed unchallenged through Sacramento airport security, were both pulled out for further inspection. We also noticed that an elderly lady was being wanded by the security person. This led me to wonder how much money could be saved if we had a security system based on common sense instead of one that considered senior citizens to be likely terrorists.

In any case, it was back to Sacramento after the dream worlds of Las Vegas and airport security. It was a nice getaway, Rome and Paris, and without having to go to Europe. It's good to be back in the "real world" of Sun City. Still, since we're going to be doing all that renovating, why not a Qua in the Fitness Center ala Caesar's Palace? I know; I'm still dreaming.

July 2008 Observations

I see I managed to mention the birth of our one and only granddaughter, Stephanie Julia Green, after having three sons and then three grandsons before her. Beverly can now have a fine time looking for girl clothes.

Observations on Why It's Good to be Retired

Every now and then, when life in retirement seems to be getting a little dull, I like to remind myself of why it's a good thing not to be working any more. So, here's the latest update. First. I don't have to worry about the I-5 "Big Fix." It was bad enough driving to downtown Sacramento (and back) even under the best of circumstances. I can just picture myself having to plot alternate routes and driving times with the "Big Fix" going on. My sympathy to those commuters who are having to cope with it. : I'm glad I'm not one of them. And speaking of commuting, I'm glad I'm no longer working so I'd have to fill up my gas tank every week at today's gas prices. When I filled up last week, I was shocked to find that a gallon of regular had gone up to $4.16 ($4.15.9) . After I'd pumped in just a little over half a tank, my cost came to over $42, a new record. Today, when I checked, the price had jumped up to about $4.50. The next time I fill up I'm sure it'll be another record.

I'm also glad I'm no longer working because, if I was, I'd have to be worried about my job in this lousy economy. Even way back when I was a State employee, we'd have budget deficits, which led to hiring freezes, then the call for 10 percent cuts (yes, Arnold, that's nothing new) and rumors of all the bad things to come would fly through the office. Now that the budget deficit is up to $15 billion and growing (good work, Arnold), I can imagine what it's like in State offices. And in the private sector I'm sure it's even worse. There, you can get thrown out at a moment's notice.

Now that Barack Obama has been nominated (although Hillary, I'm sure, will never concede) and the Democrats are favored to win, I'd be worried about my taxes going up. If I'm not mistaken, Barack has already said he'd increase the payroll tax. Then there's his determination to have government-run health insurance for all. I don't know how this will work out, but I do know that somebody will have to pay for it. Who will that somebody be? I think I also know the answer to that.

If I was still working, I'd also be concerned about my retirement. Private sector companies are cutting their retirement plans or doing away with them altogether. The baby boomers will be retiring so there's a crisis looming for Social Security, which nobody, certainly not our politicians, wants to recognize and there's no sign that anything will be done about it soon. As it is, I'm a little concerned about my own retirement now. You never know, especially with those clowns in Sacramento.

Even without all of these things, I'd still be worried if I was still working today. I have enough problems with my personal computer. What if I had to work on an office computer? First, I'd have to learn all the ins and outs of using it, which I'm sure are far more complex than in my day when PC's were just coming into use. Then, what if I hit the wrong key and lost some key piece of data? Or sent an e-mail to the wrong person (as they show on TV commercials, and then ask, Are you looking for another job?) Or what if I did something to cause my computer to crash? Or what if my computer was attacked by a virus? When I was working, I knew enough to do a few simple spread-sheets and that was sufficient. I'm glad I'm not working in my office today.

I'm also glad I'm not working because I don't have to travel under today's conditions. Way back in my day there were commuter flights from Sacramento to San Francisco, Los Angeles, San Diego and smaller cities. It was nothing to hop a plane in the morning, arrive, do your business, and be back that night. I can only wonder what it's like now. That is, if State employees are even traveling by plane any more. Even driving from Sacramento to San Francisco, once a breeze, is now, I know from recent experience, a long and tedious experience.

Another reason I'm glad to be retired is that Beverly and I have the time to visit our new granddaughter, Stephanie Julia, born June 4th, in Galway, Ireland, to our youngest son Chris and his wife Flindie. We're going there in September. Of course, we'll be seeing our grandson Logan, now 16 months, also. (See how I managed to work that in here).

Finally, I'm glad to be retired because I had time to put out another book, "Collected Stories, Volume III," available on the internet or you can contact me to see if I have any author's copies left. (I managed to work this in here, too).

August 2008 Observations:

The death of Vic Hershkowitz, the champion handball player, brought back many memories and I indulged myself by writing about some of them. I don't know how interested readers were in them; maybe they struck a chord with some ex-New Yorkers who also played handball. But that's the good thing about writing these "Observations"; I can indulge myself from time to time.

Observations on a Minor Sport

I was going to write something entirely different for this issue until last week my cousin from New York called to tell me of the death of Vic Hershkowitz. If you aren't an old handball player, you probably have never heard of Vic Hershkowitz. If you are, and especially if you're from New York City, you know that Hershkowitz was regarded by most as the best handball player of all time, having won 23 singles and doubles titles between 1947 and 1961. He also won 12 national Masters titles.

So, some of you are asking, what's handball? Handball is a game (a minor sport) that may have originated as far back as ancient Egypt. "Modern" handball is an Irish game which, according to an article I googled, was well-established in the United States by 1900. It started in Brooklyn (where Hershkowitz was born). In the 1930's, the New York City Parks Department built thousands of handball courts throughout the five boroughs. This was one-wall handball, with a wall 20' high and a court 20' by 40'. There's also three and four-wall handball. (Hershkowitz won titles in all three forms of handball and in 1952 held them all at once.)

As you'll have guessed, I'm an old handball player. Growing up in the Bronx, I was small for my age, not especially fast and wore glasses. I did have pretty good hand-eye coordination but was only fair at all the street games, notably stickball, we played. When I was 11 or 12, I got into a game of handball at the schoolyard and, what do you know, I was good at it. After I could beat all the other kids at the schoolyard, I went to Crotona Park, about a mile's walk, to find better competition; then, after a couple of years, I took the trolley to MacCombs Dam, by Yankee Stadium, where the really good players were (One of the articles on Hershkowitz's death mentions Crotona Park and MacCombs Dam as the two handball centers of the Bronx).

Participants in a minor sport tend to be fanatical. My friends and I considered handball to be the best game going. You didn't have to be big, as in baseball (or have to take steroids to get even bigger). You didn't have to be huge, as in football. You didn't have to be super-tall, as in basketball. You didn't even have to be that fast, especially in doubles. You didn't need a lot of equipment, just a pair of gloves and what we then called sneakers. You also had to use both hands, unlike tennis and other racket sports. If your off-hand was weak, you wouldn't win many games. (Herschkowitz's left hand was about as good as his right).

Remembering those old handball days, I recall the walk back from Crotona Park on a hot summer afternoon with the voice of Mel Allen, the old Yankee announcer, drifting out of open windows. I recall the candy store on the edge of the park where we used to stop in for malteds (not milk shakes), four glasses in the tin container for 25 cents. I also remember taking money for lunch, a quarter for two hot dogs and a soda at a deli.

When I started playing at MacCombs Dam, all I heard about was the great Vic Hershkowitz. I was later to see him play at the Brighton Beach Baths in Brooklyn, when I was old enough to go out there by subway. But on one memorable occasion, he showed up at MacCombs Dam. He had a manager with him to arrange the bets. Oh, yes, the top handball players played for money. He played someone singles, using his left hand, and won. He wasn't tall and he was stocky, hit the ball hard and moved like a cat. (The obituaries said he was 5 feet 8 inches and 180 pounds or so). After the singles, his manager arranged a doubles match with three of our top players. Needless to say, Herschkowitz won. I don't know why he came to our courts this one time; maybe he needed some easy money. At any rate, I was glad I was there to see him. It was like having Tiger Woods drop into our golf course. (In his obits, Herschkowitz was compared to Babe Ruth).

I think I learned a thing or two at the handball courts, aside from not playing strangers for money. In one of my first games at MacCombs Dam, I complained about the sun being in my eyes. My partner said, "The sun? Ignore it." In other words, stop your complaining; the sun's in everyone's eyes. I also learned how to win (sometimes) and how to lose (a lot) graciously, Nobody liked a blowhard and if you bragged about how good you played you were labeled a "stiff." I found out that in a game it didn't matter who a person was; the only thing that mattered was how well he played. We had people of all kinds at the courts: lawyers, judges, accountants, garment district workers, at least one bookmaker and the movie critic for one of the New York papers. No one cared. Could you play? Were you a stiff? (Hershkowitz was a New York fireman for 20 years).

My high school started a handball team in my third year there and I captained it for two years. I won a letter, something I could never have done in any other sport. After that, I went to college on a "handball scholarship"; well, maybe not technically, but the coach of our team was a graduate of that college. In reading about Hershkowitz, who was 89 when he died, in Florida, I found that handball is still alive and well at Brighton Beach. I was happy to see that. But the days of four-glass malteds and two-hot dogs-and-a-soda lunches for a quarter; well, they're nice to remember.

September 2008 Observations

More memories, this time of World War II. One thing I didn't mention was that in 1942 I had my first job, working that summer in New York's garment district as a stock and delivery boy for a buttons wholesaler. I had to join a union, made sixty cents an hour and clutched my first check, $24, in my hand all the way on the subway ride back home from work so that nobody would steal it. Of course, I gave the check to my mother.

Observations Looks Back at WWII

Last month's Observations were inspired by learning of the death of Vic Hershkowitz, possibly the best handball player of all time, and a boyhood idol of mine in the 1940's. A lot of memories of this period came flooding back, so I've decided to devote this month's column to some recollections of World War II, which, if any younger readers come across this, was 1941-1945.

Unlike the current "war on terror," which may be real but seems remote from the ordinary lives of most of us, WWII touched the lives of all Americans. My father, who'd served in the Navy after WWI, was too old to serve in WWII. Nevertheless, the war had a major impact of his life and thus on the lives of our family. In 1939, two years before the start of the war, and after struggling to find enough work (he was a plumber) during the Depression years, he first left New York City to go into "defense work" in Florida. He then went to such places as Oklahoma, Wisconsin, Michigan and Oak Ridge, Tennessee (where he worked in the plant making the atomic bomb). Nowadays, the absence of a father for all this time would have meant doom for our family. Luckily, in those days psychiatrists and psychologists were not all over the place to tell us this, so we went on with our lives and survived.

The war meant shortages on the "home front," as we were known, and I'm pretty sure, without looking it up, that we had ration books for certain items, gas for one. I've just looked it up and tires were the first item to be rationed as the supply of natural rubber was cut off. For me and my fellow handball players at Crotona Park in the Bronx tires didn't matter, but what did matter was that the good old rubber Spalding (pronounced "Spaldeen") balls we were used to playing with were a wartime casualty. Instead, we had to make do with balls made from "ersatz" rubber, which didn't bounce very well and tended to come apart in two halves after only a few games.

World War II might have had an even more drastic effect on our family. One summer my father was working in Midland, Michigan and my mother, my sister and I went out there to stay with him in a little house he'd found. I guess we just left our apartment in the Bronx as it was. This was the first time any of us, except for my father, had been on a train and the first time we'd been outside of New York City. As I recall, we kind of liked living in a small town. We went to an early supermarket, the A&P, to shop. I recall going to watch the local softball team play at night. We even went fishing once and I have a picture of myself and my sister holding up a string of fish to prove it.

The one bad thing about Midland was that a Dow Chemical plant was there, and the taste and smell of the chemicals, was in everything, the food, the air, the water. At that time people weren't aware that they were at risk for cancer. The people in Midland all liked my father, as everyone did wherever he went, and they offered many inducements for us to buy that small house and stay there. Fortunately, my mother resisted; and at the end of the summer, we took the train back to New York. I wonder about our life expectancies had we stayed in Midland, and about what happened to the people we met there that summer.

The war pervaded all aspects of life. At school, we bought war stamps, which could then be converted into war bonds. If I recall correctly, $18.75 got you a war bond, which would then pay you $25 after I don't know how many years. So war bonds were a favorite present for relatives to give kids. People collected scrap iron. Women went to work and Rosie the riveter was born. Songwriters wrote songs about the war; someone called Spike Jones sang about "der Fuehrer's face and Kate Smith sang "God Bless America." In the movies, Nazis were the favorite villains. Most war movies were probably pretty bad, but one of them was "Casablanca."

After D-Day, we knew that America and its allies would win the war, but the end didn't come until 1945. V-E Day was May 8th, signifying the end of the war in Europe. V-J Day was August 14th, the end of the war against Japan. For my family, the war didn't feel over until two or three years after that when there was a building boom in New York and my father was finally able to leave his last out-of-town job and come home.

October 2008 Observations---Looks for a Worthy Subject

Every month I have to think of a subject for Observations. For the last two months, I've looked back at the 1940's, the World War II years. This month I thought I'd get back to the present. So, what to write about?

The John Edwards story has just popped up in the news, in the media other than the National Inquirer anyway. Married politician has affair with woman. Nothing very new in that. To be sure, there are a few wrinkles in this particular story. Married politician's wife has cancer. He ran for vice-president and was running for the presidential nomination. He hired the woman to work for his campaign. The National Inquirer says he fathered the woman's baby. But basically it's the same old thing, and as always the talking heads on cable TV have said all the same old things, including the startling statements that we're all human and that everyone does it. My only observation is that I'm always amazed about how sincerely politicians can lie. And, Edwards does have nice hair. So, let's dismiss the Edwards' affair.

There's the ongoing election story, but hasn't this been going on forever? During the primaries, wasn't everyone asking, What will Hillary do? And now they're asking, what will Hillary do at the convention? And after the primaries, wasn't this supposed to be a civil, respectful debate on the issues? No, I didn't believe it either. So let's pass on the election.

What about the California budget impasse? Hasn't this been going on forever, also? And doesn't this happen every year? Governor Arnold has added a new wrinkle, fire temporary and part-time State workers and cut everyone's pay. Still, it's pretty much the same old story: when the state has more than enough money the politicians can't wait to spend it all, then when the money stops coming in there's a budget crisis. Let's move on.

What about $4 a gallon gas? Wait a minute, the price of oil has been going down and so gas is, as of this writing, actually under $4 a gallon. And I didn't even have a chance to inflate my tires and have a tune-up. So what now, does this mean we don't have to start drilling for oil after all and that people can go back to buying SUV's. You got me. I'll pass on this one, too.

Sports are usually good for a story. The Olympics are on, but as usual the television coverage is terrible (you never really know what event is on when, and anyway the event is usually over by the time it airs), the little Chinese gymnasts (female) are obviously, some of them, underage but nobody wants to make a fuss about it, the usual stuff. I'd like to see

Michael Phelps win his eight golds and I'd like to see the American basketball team win it all, but otherwise nothing to get excited about.

So what to write about? I'd like to forget about politicians, elections, budget battles, the bad economy, sports figures, celebrities, entertainers, TV anchors and all others who make those ridiculously inflated salaried, and this month recognize some of the people who really do matter. These would include: doctors and nurses who truly care about their patients, EMI's, teachers who truly care about their profession; scientists working in labs somewhere who'll uncover cures for diseases; technicians who are figuring out how to get at energy sources, whatever they are---fossil fuels, wind, air, solar---while the politicians are busy pontificating and pointing their fingers at one another; firemen; ambulance drivers, librarians; the people who do all those jobs we never think about, like fast-food chain waitresses, chambermaids, bellboys, dishwashers; even those State employees who try to do a good job and whose pay Governor Arnold wants to cut.

Let's also recognize the people who volunteer at the SPCA, who deliver meals-on-wheels, who work as unpaid docents, as well as individuals, such as those here in Sun City, who care for neighbors who are ill or have suffered accidents, who collect their neighbors' mail or take out their garbage when needed. And people who help others carry packages to their cars, who return objects we may have dropped or forgotten; people who offer a friendly smile. As I finish this column, the political conventions are about to start. As we watch these staged events, let's think about the genuine people who, while the politicians and pundits are sounding off, really make the world work.

November 2008 Observations

I first became aware of the impending financial crisis in the United States while visiting our son and his family in Ireland. When we returned, the financial markets really imploded. As we now know, the result was our Recession, the worst in a long time, although not the Great Depression some "experts" told us was coming. If the financial news at the time was all bad though at least I could receive it while sitting in my comfortable Lazy-Boy and I could always take refuge in a nice hot shower.

Observations on Returning from Ireland

It's happened again. Beverly and I recently (in September) spent three weeks in Ireland, visiting our son Chris, his wife Flindie, our year-and-a-half old grandson Logan and our new (four-months-old) granddaughter Stephanie. Before we left, things seemed to be fairly normal, i.e., California was still struggling to pass a budget, O.J. Simpson was about to go to trial, there was a presidential election which had been going on forever, the usual stuff. In our absence, you know what happened. Wall Street banking houses failed: Fanny Mae and Freddie Mac were taken over; then, while we were getting over jet lag, came the big on-again, off-again bailout (or "rescue"), followed by a plunge in the stock market and fears of a worldwide recession.

No, I'm not about to add to the all of the million of words already said about the current financial mess by assorted pundits and "experts." Instead, I thought I'd note down some of the things I didn't miss while in Ireland and some I did. First, I didn't miss the above-mentioned never-ending presidential campaign. After a while in Ireland, I realized that I hadn't heard the names John McCain and Barack Obama for three whole days and that was a relief. When we returned and I started watching the cable "news" channels to catch up on things, I realized I hadn't missed the unending back-and-forth natterings of what someone called the "gasbags" on TV.

Aside from the above, I hadn't missed all of the junk mail that was piled up high on our kitchen table when we got back. When faced with three weeks' worth of this stuff, it's incredible how much all of the outfits that want your money send out. Maybe if they didn't spend so much money on printing and mailing their material they wouldn't need so much money. I also didn't miss the spam that appeared on my computer every day. I'd deleted some spam while checking my e-mail using my son's computer, but there was still a lot left and they were all the same old things sent over and over again.

I also didn't miss the doctor and dental appointments that are an inevitable part of a senior citizen's calendar. My doctor wanted to see me because he was worried about my blood pressure, which is always high when I'm in his office and usually normal at all other times. My dentist wanted to see me because it was time for my next check-up to see how much worse my teeth had gotten since the last check-up. It was also time for the annual flu shot, which might help fight off the next season's flu, or possibly give me the flu, or not do anything one way or the other.

There were, however, certain things I found I did miss when away. First and foremost, I missed good old American plumbing. The apartment we stayed in had a notice on the bathroom wall that warned not to flush the toilet within 20 minutes of taking a shower. The shower itself was one of those complicated European contraptions that looked as if it had been devised by a mad scientist. It was also hand-held so you couldn't just stand under it and the water, whether you flushed the toilet or not, was never more than lukewarm.

I also missed my lazy-boy chair. The furniture in our son's house and in our apartment was comfortable enough, but I've become accustomed to putting up my foot rest and leaning back in my chair and it felt good to do that when we returned. And even though our local newspaper leaves a lot to be desired, I was glad to turn to the sports pages and see baseball and football instead of soccer and cricket.

I started writing this a few days ago and in that time the above-mentioned financial mess has gotten even worse. Even if we went back to Ireland we couldn't escape as it's a global phenomenon and Ireland has guaranteed the deposits of its major banks. Think I'll turn off the financial channel, take a nice hot shower and retire to my lazy-boy chair to read the sports page.

December 2008 Observations

I noted in this "Observations" that our country had swung back to liberalism after a period of conservatism and also noted that things don't always proceed that neatly. As I write this, Obama and the Democrats are still intent on their liberal agenda, but Republican candidates have been winning elections. We'll see where the country stands after the November elections.

On a more personal note, I still think new beginnings are a good thing for people. My latest new beginning has been to take a drawing class and to try my hand at pen-and-ink sketching. Some people might not think that's a good thing for the art world, but I'm having fun.

Observations on New Beginnings

As this is being written in the aftermath of an election in which the candidate for change prevailed it seems an appropriate time to consider the subject of "new beginnings." Since its inception, America has been a country of new beginnings. The early colonists came here from Europe to find new beginnings for their lives. As the country expanded, it was common for people to "go West" to start new lives for themselves. Even now we believe in second chances, that people aren't stuck in bad situations, that they can make new beginnings for themselves.

For the families of many of us, a new beginning was, like the early colonists, coming to America from countries where they were either oppressed or lacked opportunity. My father's father came here from Poland during the Spanish-American War when tailors were needed to sew uniforms for the Army. My mother was brought over as a baby from Hungary.

After World War II, many servicemen who'd been stationed in California or who'd just passed through, followed the old dictum to "go West" and relocated to a state where, in most places, you didn't have to shovel snow in the winter, and where you could buy a home. I suppose you could say that I too made a new beginning by coming out to California from New York City (after the Korean War, not WWII). .

I think it's fair to say that most of us who live in Sun City made a new beginning, late in our lives, by leaving the places where we'd lived during our working years and where we'd raised our families to come to a retirement community. I'd already made a new beginning after retiring by becoming a free-lance writer for the Neighbors section (remember that?) of the Sacramento Bee. Another new beginning was becoming a writer for the Sun Senior News. Meanwhile, my wife Beverly made a new beginning by becoming a watercolor artist whose paintings are hanging in many Sun City houses. I'm sure almost every reader has his or hers new beginnings story, whether it's serving on a committee, becoming a volunteer or taking up golf.

So trying something new, even at a later age, is something which, I would say, is a good thing for us. In the last few years, Beverly and I have made a new beginning as grandparents and that has certainly been rewarding. The historian Arthur Schlesinger, Jr. saw America as undergoing cycles from liberalism to conservatism and back again. We are about to enter a new cycle, presumably back to liberalism, although things don't work that neatly. Nixon established relations with China and Clinton enacted welfare reform, so you never know.

It was obvious that the country wanted a change. President-elect Obama recognized this early on and, on a platform of change, was elected. I believe the desire for change was at least in part a generational thing. When I look at Obama, I see an awfully young guy. Of course, this is true when I look at a lot of people. My three sons were all enthusiasts for him. Obama has such a thin record that it's hard to tell what his "change" will turn out to be. Also, events have a way of overtaking political programs. e.g., September 11th.

Setting out on a new beginning can be scary. I imagine my father's father was a little (maybe a lot) scared when he and his family left Poland. But I'm sure he had hope for the future and that hope was stronger than his fear. As the country sets out on a new beginning, let's start out with that same spirit of hope.

2009 OBSERVATIONS

January 2009 Observations

With the current tough economic times and the constant media outcry of recession, recession, I find that my mind is turning toward the real Depression days of the 1930's. I was born in 1929 (after the stock market crash, so I'm not to blame) so, like many Sun City residents, I'm sure, grew up during this era. . In my case, my father, a plumber, mother and later my sister and I lived in a tenement in the Bronx (New York). Our tenement apartment had a kitchen, a living room, a bathroom and two bedrooms. When my sister appeared, we shared one bedroom.

I was too young to know very much that was going on, but I did realize that jobs were hard to find. I recall that my father used to go every morning to the union hall and that most days there was no work to be had. I also knew that my father did jobs in the buildings owned by our tenement landlord. I assume that this paid, or at least helped to pay, our rent. Eventually, my father obtained work with the WPA and I know that he worked on the monument built in Herald Square, across from Macy's. I also know that the WPA put up all the handball courts in New York City parks, including the ones my friends and I played on. So, as far as I'm concerned, there's nothing wrong with government-sponsored jobs.

Even though my father didn't have steady employment and I knew this wasn't good I never felt that we were "poor': neither did any of the other kids on our block. Maybe one reason for this was that we didn't have all of those consumer goodies that everyone has now.

This was before television, if the kids nowadays can imagine there was such a time. We had a radio, and this supplied our evening's entertainment, with programs such as Jack Benny, Fred Allen, Edgar Bergen and Charlie McCarthy, The Shadow and The Inner Sanctum (remember that squeaking door?). Needless to say, we didn't have a car; nobody we knew had one. We went to places by subway, at that time costing a nickel.

Nobody we knew lived in a house. Our apartment's heat was provided by steam radiators. That is, when we had heat; when we didn't, we banged on the radiators. The only air-conditioning we knew was in the movies. Eating out? Sometimes we went to the local deli: hot dogs were, if I recall correctly, a nickel or at most a dime. I guess there just weren't a lot of things whose loss would have made us feel deprived.

I mentioned that a subway ride cost a nickel and hot dogs a nickel or a dime. Another reason we didn't feel poor, at least we kids didn't, is that things didn't cost that much. A penny was actually worth something. It would buy something at a candy store. Two pennies would buy more. For a nickel, you could buy a soda or an ice cream. An ice cream sundae cost, I think, fifteen cents. The ultimate in ice cream, a banana split, could be had at a Woolworth's for a quarter. Of course, you could get all sorts of things at Woolworth's, otherwise known as the five-and-dime. Of crucial importance to kids, you could buy a rubber ball for a nickel. This was a major investment so you tried to make the ball last as long as possible.

Although we didn't feel deprived, my friends and I knew that as soon as we turned thirteen and could get a work permit we did so and that summer we tried to get jobs. My first summer job was as a delivery and stockroom boy for a wholesale button place located, as it happened, across from Macy's at Herald Square. You can be sure I told everyone that my father, who by then was working out of town in war plants, had worked on the monument there.

Still another reason why we didn't feel weighed down by living in a Depression was, I think, that the media, such as it was then, wasn't all-invasive. We weren't constantly being bombarded by pundits telling us that things would get worse before they would get better, that the sky was falling in, that this was the worst time since the Great Depression. We were in the Great Depression, and somehow we survived it.

February 2009 Observations

Things looked pretty bad at the start of last year, 2009. Since then at least the stock market made a recovery; I don't know if anything else is any better. I'd add to my suggestions: eat some chocolate; eat some ice cream. Somehow we'll survive.

Observations on How to Survive the Recession

Our home prices have plummeted. The stock market is down. The economy is in a shambles. Everyone wants a bailout. The country (and the world) is in a recession. What to do? Observations offers some steps to take to get through all of this.

First, a couple of thngs NOT to do. Do not tune into CNN or any other business channel. All you'll get is a bunch of people yelling at each other and you'll learn nothing. Also, do NOT watch any of the cable news channels. All you'll get is a another bunch of people yelling at each other and a lot of misinformation. If you must watch these cable channels, do so for five minutes and then turn them off. Notice how nice and quiet it is.

Now, things to do. Start off the morning by turning to the comics and read Peanuts. If you don't get the morning paper, buy one of the Peanuts books.

Weather permitting, take a walk. Look for ducks, herons and egrets. You're bound to see some Canadian geese.

If you don't have one, get a cat. Stroking a cat will soothe your nerves. If you don't like cats (and how could this be?) then get a dog. This will mean you have to take walks (see above).

Listen to music, not the stuff they have today, but real music. Listen to some of the old musicals of the 1950's: Oklahoma, The King and I, Carousel, Pal Joey, My Fair Lady, Show Boat, Guys and Dolls.

Go to the Sun City library. It's one of our best amenities. If you live in Sun City Roseville, go to the Martha Riley public library. It's only five minutes down the road (on Pleasant Grove Boulevard). Read a book by P.D. James. She's the British mystery writer who's still going strong at 88 years old. Read a book by her friend Ruth Rendell, another British mystery writer also still going strong at age 80.

Read Shakespeare, or better, get a DVD of one of Shakespeare's plays; they're meant to be seen. Whatever it is---comedy, drama, tragedy, melodrama---and whatever it's about---love, hatred, jealousy, trust, betrayal---or whomever it's about---kings, queens, princesses, ordinary people, wise men, fools, heroes, villains---Shakespeare has written about it better than anyone before or since. .

Get the DVD of "The Wizard of Oz" and watch it again. Judy Garland, Ray Bolger, Bert Lahr, Jack Haley, Frank Morgan, "Somewhere Over the Rainbow," munchkins, witches (good and bad), flying monkeys, talking trees---what more could you want?

Go to the Fitness Center. Exercise. Walk on the treadmill. Pump iron

Go to the Waffle Barn for breakfast; best waffles in Roseville. Or, go to the Timbers for the buffet breakfast. I'm told it's really good, and a bargain. Also, go to the Timbers for the Monday and/or Thursday night bargain specials. If you're feeling flush, have dinner at La Provence. Their fixed price dinner is about $20 You say this will undo the benefits of going to the Fitness Center. Aim to break even.

If you've been meaning to go on that trip, do it. You have to go while you can.

Go through your financial and personal papers and get them all in order. This won't make your taxes any lower. But it will make you feel organized.

Go through your closets. If you haven't worn an article of clothing the last three years, give it to some charity so somebody in need can use it.

Remember: all's well that ends well. Shakespeare says so.

March 2009 Observations---Looks at Sports

As I write, the latest Super Bowl is just over so it seems an appropriate time for Observations to look at sports. My wife Beverly can't understand the attraction of sporting events. When I have one on the television, which isn't any more than 20 hours a week, all she sees are sweaty grunting people doing incomprehensible things. I wonder if other Sun City wives have the same problem. No matter, Observations will explain the appeal of sports to us guys.

First of all, sports, unlike "reality" shows and almost everything else on TV, are, like the rest of actual life, unpredictable. When you watch a sports event, you don't know from the start how it's going to turn out. (Okay, when the Kings played the Celtics, among other teams, recently you had a pretty good idea of who would win but even so the seemingly impossible sometimes happens; remember that one game the Kings beat the Lakers). I was sad after this year's Super Bowl because I can no longer say "the defending Super Bowl champions, the New York Giants " The Giants, against all odds, managed to upset the New England Patriots, a team that hadn't lost a game all year, while the Giants had been soundly beaten in several games, not to mention losing to the same Patriots in the last game of the regular season. This year's Super Bowl was almost as exciting. The favored Pittsburgh Steelers won but not until the underdog Arizona Cardinals had overcome a 13-point deficit and led until the last minute of the game.

Although sport event results are unpredictable, each event has a story line or lines which gives it suspense, drama and meaning. Would the Patriots be able to go through the season unbeaten, something no NFL team had been able to do since the Miami Dolphins years ago? Would the Giants' quarterback Eli Manning be able to hold together in the biggest of all games? Would the Steelers become the first team to win six Super Bowls? Could the much-derided Cardinals (only 9-7 in the regular season) stay on the same field with the Steelers? On Super Bowl Sunday, ESPN showed the final (taped) match of the Australian Open men's final, between number-one ranked Rafael Nadal and number-two Roger Federer. Here the drama was: could Federer win his 14th major title, typing him with Pete Sampras? Could Nadal, unbeatable on a clay court, beat Federer on a hard court? The match went to five sets before Federer finally weakened and Nadal won. After the match, when the trophies were presented, Federer couldn't control his emotions and cried. He'd come so close. Now the drama continues at the next major tournament, the French Open.

Other dramas in sports: could the cursed Red Sox finally win a World Series? They did. Could the Boston Celtics, after years of futility, recover some of their lost glory and win another NBA championship? They did. Could Pete Sampras, after an indifferent year, reach back and win his 14th major tournament at the U.S. Open? He did. Each of these story lines had a satisfying conclusion. Can any TV drama match these? My answer would be "No."

Another appeal of sports is that fans identify with teams. Sometimes these are their old college or high school teams, but most of the time they are the teams representing their cities, such as our Sacramento Kings. Such identification can go too far, for example, those fans shown at Oakland Raider games. As the saying goes, fans live or die with their teams. Even if, as with the current Kings, it's mostly dying, the good thing is that people are connected with something larger than themselves and outside of their ordinary lives. Wait, does this sound like religion? Well, to some die-hard fans, sports can be a religion.

One final element in the appeal of sports is that we are able to watch top-flight athletes doing amazing things. I mentioned watching the Australian Open tennis final. This was on tape so I knew who won. Still, as a one-time tennis player (hacker), it was fascinating to watch the two top players in the game make shots, cover the court and hold rallies whose difficulty I had at least some idea of. I might add that when a rare butchered shot is made it's comforting that even players like Nadal and Federer can be guilty of doing what we hackers do every time we play.

There are undoubtedly other reasons for sports' appeal to people. I hope I've given some glimpse of why us guys sit in front of our TV sets watching those sweaty grunting athletes.

April 2009 Observations

The half dozen or so faithful readers of this column must occasionally wonder how I'm able to turn out an Observations month after month, year after year, etc. Okay, maybe you couldn't care less, but I'm going to tell you anyway. The first step of course is to sit down in front of the computer. The next step is to turn the computer on. This is the signal for our cat Shandyman to suddenly appear out of nowhere and jump on the back of my computer chair, his cat ESP having told him that his master (ha!) was about to attempt doing some work. After stroking Shandyman and shooing him off, it occurs to me that I'd better take a look at the Smartmoney website to see what the stock market is doing today.

Connecting to the Internet should be a quick and simple process as I have Comcast and you've probably seen those commercials where a turtle complains that Comcast is too fast for him. I think that Comcast has heard the turtle's complaint and has slowed down to accommodate him. At any rate, it seems to take hours to finally be connected. I note this down as one of life's little annoyances (LLA's) for a future Observations. When I look at Smartmoney I see that stocks are down, no surprise there, but by less than 100, so this might be a good day.

Time to get started. I type Observations at the top of the page. There's a little ding and I see that I've gotten an e-mail. Have to take a look. Maybe it's an e-zine editor telling me that one of my stories has been accepted. No, it's one of those e-mails telling me I've won another lottery Somehow it slipped past the Spam filter. Another LLA to note down.

Reminded of Spam, I look at my Spam folder and see that my Spam folder is now up to almost 500. Maybe it's so filled up that's why the lottery e-mail wasn't put there. One of these days I'll have to look at the folder and clear it out. Maybe I'll do an Observations on it and note that all of the e-mails demanding an URGENT REPLY are invariably from people with names usually associated with terrorist organizations. Well, maybe Al-Queda does have an urgent message for me. If so, it'll have to wait.

Time to get started, again. On cue, the phone rings. I pick it up and say, "Hello." Nothing. "Hello, hello. Is anyone there?" Still nothing. It's one of those "no one's there calls" that come three or four times every day. Another LLA. Make a note. My eye falls on the calendar. Uh, oh, it's the eighth of the month, the deadline for sending things to the Courier, and I've completely forgotten about it. I save the Observations, a blank page except for "Observations" typed at the top of it, and quickly dash off the meeting announcement I have to send in. That's done anyway.

Time to type the first sentence of my Observations. I recently came upon an old book of pieces by the incomparable humorist Robert Benchley, who was a master of writing something about nothing. That'll do it. By now you've grasped the secret of writing a monthly Observations. You sit down at your computer and, letting nothing distract you, type one word after another. Before you know it, you have a column.

P.S. For this month, I wanted to do something different and a little Benchleyesque. For the real thing go to the book store or the library and try to find something by him. If you can't, because he wrote in the prehistoric days when I was still a kid, get something by Dave Barry, who's more recent. Well, a good morning's work: stroked Shandyman, got the Courier thing in, steered my faithful half dozen readers to some really good reading and finished another Observations. Maybe the next one will be on LLA's. Time for a well-deserved lunch.

May 2009 Observations---on Sun City (Updated)

As readers know, Observations occasionally takes time off from solving the problems of the world to take a look at what's going on in Sun City. As this is being written, Sun City Roseville is about to celebrate "Spirit Days," so this would seem to be an appropriate time to take such a look. Apologies in advance to SCLH readers; the writer lives in SCR so his observations are necessarily based on what he sees here. I'm sure many of the comments about SCR can also apply to SCLH. In any case, SCLH readers are invited to let me know what they think of their Sun City.

To get down to it, Observations thinks that living in Sun City is better than ever. For one thing, now that our trees and shrubbery have matured, it looks much better. When Beverly and I first moved here, we were a bit worried that Sun City had a sterile look. We needn't have worried. It's now pleasant to walk around the neighborhood streets as well as the public places. It's nice that a variety of wildlife have found Sun City and made it their home---doves, quail, herons, egrets, ducks, jackrabbits, chipmunks and even our friends the Canadian geese. (We'll have even more wildlife when the golf course is converted to a nature area. Oh, wait, that was an April Fool's joke. Relax, golfers.)

SCR's Timbers restaurant has had its ups and downs over the years. I think the recent menu innovations with their more than reasonable prices have given the restaurant a new spark, not to mention greatly increasing the number of people eating there. Beverly and I have been there for a few dinners. What impressed me most was, with the restaurant jampacked, how fast and efficient the service was. (A little nitpick: I wish they had sugar on the tables to begin with as every time I order ice tea I forget to ask for it and then have to flag down a server to bring it.)

Another improvement is SCR's monthly newsletter, the Courier, which now is in color and looks much more like a magazine than a newsletter. Of course, the Courier, though much improved, doesn't have "Favorite Restaurants" or "Observations", which are in the monthly Sun Senior News. Fortunately, Sun City residents also get the Sun Senior News, delivered through the mail at no cost, so they have the best of both worlds.

By the time this appears, the newly renovated Fitness Center will have opened and I'm sure will be an improvement. Further down the line, the new Sierra Pines should rectify one of

SCR's deficiencies, not having an adequate clubhouse. The library has always been a great SCR amenity. I don't think it's changed too much since we've been here (readers, correct me if I'm wrong) but then it's always been good as far as I'm concerned. SCR residents are also fortunate in now having the Martha Riley public library only a few minutes' drive away.

One last thing and maybe it doesn't exactly tie in with the above, but probably because we've just lost an old and dear friend, I've been thinking of Sun City friends and neighbors who have passed on. Most readers, like myself, have probably gone to more than one memorial service since living here. Time then passes, life goes on, and memories fade. How to remember? A few cases in point. The first thing that came to mind was the Vietnam memorial. Then I recalled that when we first moved here Beverly and I donated a brick with our names inscribed to a Roseville park then opening. Finally, the Maui hotel where our son Michael married his wife Bridget has a walkway with stones inscribed with bride and bridegroom names on them. It doesn't have to be elaborate, but maybe Sun City could have something commemorating residents who are no longer with us. Maybe we can even have one day a year when we remember them, a Sun City Memorial Day. Okay, just a thought. Any comments?

June 2009 Observations---on TGH's (Once Again)

As everyone knows, or should know, some things are guaranteed to happen, like California failing to pass a budget by the required time every year or some celebrity going into rehab or the Kings …let's not get into that. Here are some things that are guaranteed to happen while you are living in Sun City.

Your garage door will malfunction. This will happen on a Friday night or over a weekend. Your air-conditioner will stop working, during a heat wave in summer, and on a Friday night or over a weekend. Your furnace will stop working, during the coldest spell in winter, on a Friday night or over (you know the rest). Your drip system or one of your sprinklers will stop working or somehow malfunction. You'll be going on a cruise the next day.

At some time, you won't close your car door all the way or some interior light will be on and you won't notice it and the next morning your battery (and car) will be dead. I don't have to tell you when this will happen. At some point, you'll put something on top of your car just temporarily, or maybe on top of your trunk, then you'll forget about it and drive away. You'll see a space in the Sun City parking lot, then find there's a golf cart in it. One day, or night, you'll forget where you left your car in the parking lot, maybe even the Sun City parking lot.

At some time you'll go to a meeting and find you had the wrong day or maybe the wrong week. At another time when the meeting is at someone's house you'll go to the wrong house. At some point you won't be able to find your car key, or your wallet, or the TV remote. You'll search all over and find the missing object in some unlikely place. At some point, you'll forget and leave a credit card in a store or a restaurant and have to call and rush over to retrieve it. This will also happen with a cap or a jacket. You'll also lose a library book and lose or misplace your Sun City ID card.

While watching a TV program you'll recognize an actor or actress you've seen in some other program but you won't be able to remember what. This might keep you up all night. Tip: Google it. At some point, you won't be able to remember the TV program or the movie you've just seen or the book you've just read. Don't worry about it, happens to everybody.

You'll have a trip all planned out and something will happen. You'll go on a trip and miss your plane or your plane will be delayed. No matter what, you'll have to take your shoes off at the airport (a GTH). You'll have called and asked that your newspaper be stopped and when you return your doorstep will be piled high with newspapers.

You'll be waiting for an important call, the phone rings and it's someone else. Someone will call and address you by your first name. It'll be nobody you know, only somebody asking you to upgrade your credit card or to donate to a worthy cause. You'll want to get on your computer for some important e-mail or other task and discover it's not working. You'll call technical support and a person with an accent you can barely understand will tell you to disconnect and then re-connect your computer. It still won't work.

One morning you'll wake up with a pain in your arm or leg or back or somewhere. You'll have no idea where it came from. One year you'll have some major dental work, a crown or a root canal or worse. The cost, high, won't be covered by your dental insurance, if you have any. One time something will happen to you, your wife or a friend, and you'll have to go to a hospital emergency room. You'll have to wait a long, long time. You'll get a winter cold. You'll get a summer cold. Whatever malady you come down with, everyone you know will have had it already, only worse.

You'll send an e-mail with an attachment and forget to attach. If you're reading this, it means I remembered this time.

July 2009 Observations

Last month's Observations was about TGH's, Things Guaranteed to Happen, while living in Sun City. Since then Beverly and I have gone on a river cruise through Holland and Belgium. It was a good trip, but like all such tours, it had some down moments, starting with the unpleasant necessity that, if you want to get from Sun City to Amsterdam, you have to fly there. So this month will be an Observations on TGH's when going on such a trip.

Let's skip over the security aspects of today's air travel, with its TGH of having to take off your shoes and all the rest of it, and get on the plane. The first GTH is that the space between seats has shrunk so much that you barely have any leg room and you have to be a contortionist to either get in or out. The next GTH is that as soon as the plane takes off the person in front of you will lower his (or her) seat so that it's almost in your lap. Sooner or later you'll want to get up and use the airplane facility. It's a GTH that you and your wife will be in the window and middle seats and that the passenger in the aisle seat will be a large person who'll fall asleep as soon as he sits down. So getting up and out means waking up this large person, making your apologies, and then slithering your way to freedom, only to find, almost a sure-fire GTH, that your way is locked by a flight attendant with a food cart.

The never-ending flight finally over, you disembark and, discover, to your relief, that your bags have made it. Also to your relief, someone from your tour company meets you, rounds up all the other tour members and herds you to a waiting van. At this point, all you want to do is get to your hotel and collapse. Sure enough, the van has to wait for that one couple in every tour group that can't be found. Maybe it's the same couple that couldn't be found on your last trip.

The missing couple is finally found and you make it to your hotel, but once the trip is safely underway, there are a few more GTH's waiting to happen. You're bound to lose something---a hat, a coat, an umbrella, with luck not a wallet or a camera. In my case, I have a propensity for losing caps, which is why I now always carry a spare. Several caps of mine, an Atlantic Braves one and a Kings one, are floating somewhere around Europe. Let me know if you see either one on your next trip. Also, something is bound to break. My eyeglasses, for example, seem to develop a fatal weakness when they get abroad and crack in the middle or have one of the little screws come out. This never happens when I'm home, only in a country where the opticians don't speak English.

Another GTH on a tour is that no matter where you're going you must leave no later than 9 AM. If you're in a big city and going to see some churches and museums the bus leaves at 9 AM. If you're in a small town the walking tour leaves at 9 AM. It's also a GTH that, no matter where you're going, one, usually quite a few, of your tour group will be asking everyone else, what time do we leave again?

Another tour GTH is that someone in the group will be the designated complainer (No, it wasn't me; I didn't say anything until we got home and I wrote this column). The designated complainer will complain about anything: the weather, the hotel room, the ship's cabin, the food, the prices. Sometimes the complaint can be a little strange. On this trip we had a "Dutch" lunch out, just ham and cheese and rolls. One lady complained because we weren't given serrated knives to cut the rolls. That's reaching about as far as you can go for a complaint.

The final GTH about a trip like this is that no matter what the complaints and no matter how many down moments, after you've returned home and have finally gotten over your jet-lag you forget about all the bad things and assure all your friends that the everything was great. .

August 2009 Observations

Maybe it goes along with aging, but I find that more and more I'm glad to get home after a trip. Travel is fine but it can also be tiring, and then there's the ever increasing hassle of flying (see "Observations" on the Holland/Belgium cruise above). And at home you can take your afternoon nap.

Observations on Why There's No Place Like Home

"There's no place like home. There's no place like home. There's no place like home." Dorothy said it in "The Wizard of Oz" and I tend to agree with her. As mentioned here last month,

Beverly and I recently went on a river cruise from Amsterdam through Holland and Belgium. We enjoyed the cruise and it was good to get away for a while. Beds made up by the cabin steward. Eggs cooked to order every morning as we breakfasted in the ship's restaurant. Sumptuous lunches and dinners, complete with desserts. No doctor or dentist appointments. No junk mail. No spam. What a life! Still, we were glad when we got back.

Our accommodations, both hotel and cruise ship, were good. But, let's face it, there's nothing like coming home and being able to sleep in your own bed again, even if there's no cabin steward to make it up. You have your own real pillows. You have your own mattress, which has adjusted to your body's contours. It's also nice to sit in your own chair again, especially if it's a lazy-boy chair. No matter how comfortable other chairs may be, there's nothing like a lazy-boy. You can lean back, put up the foot rest and stretch out all you want. You might fall asleep, but that's okay, too. It's even nicer when one of your cats sits in your lap. All right, your cats may not have rushed out to greet you (they're not dogs), but you know they're glad that you're back.

It's also nice to have a morning newspaper to go with your breakfast, even if it's the attenuated Bee that's barely half its old size. It still has a sports section and the sports are American ones like baseball and basketball, not rugby and cricket as in the overseas papers. In a way it's also good to see the same old news again. California has a budget crisis, legislators can't agree, Governor Arnold is as buffoonish as ever---somehow, it's reassuring that some things never change.

It's even reassuring, at least for a while (maybe a very short while) to see the same old cable TV "news" programs. Yes, the same pundits are still making the same pronouncements with complete confidence, no matter how many times they've been wrong before. The same politicians are still dishing out the same old lies with absolute conviction. The same talking heads are still yelling at each other. Ah, yes, good old American TV; there's nothing like it. Good thing you can always turn it off.

Although you've eaten like a king on your trip, it's good to get back to American food. MacDonald's is popular all over Holland and Belgium, but there's nothing like a real made-in-America hamburger. It's also nice that in American restaurants the servers will bring you water with ice in it, most of the time without your having to ask. And you don't have to pay extra for it. It's good to get back to your computer, even with all the spam that's accumulated on it during your absence. It's also nice to catch up on your mail, despite all the junk in it. Every now and then you might get something worthwhile. You can hope anyway.

Of course, I've left the best part of returning home for last, you re-connect with your friends and family, especially your grandchildren. And your cats. Yes, it's good to be back. There's no place like home; that is, until you're ready to go off on your next trip. Then the cycle starts up all over again.

September 2009 Observations---Asks Some Questions

In the very first Observations, many years ago, I posed the question: the parking lot at the Lodge is almost always full but when you go inside the Lodge it's empty, so where does everyone go? I'm still looking for a satisfactory answer to this question; if any reader has one please let me know. Meanwhile, a few other questions about things that continue to puzzle.

The recent California budget battle as usual centered on the state's education system, which keeps on getting the lion's share of the State's money yet never seems to have enough and whose results never seem to be too good. Whenever this comes up I can't help but think back to my own schooldays (and this was many, many, many years ago) when we didn't have any of today's computers and other technical aids, just a pencil box, and still everyone managed to learn how to read and write and do arithmetic. We also had geography and most kids knew where the countries of the world were. We had history and most kids knew about George Washington and the Revolutionary War, Abraham Lincoln and the Civil War, even about the first World War. So how come today's kids can't seem to learn even the basics, can't read, can't spell, don't know where Canada is and don't know what Pearl Harbor was? Answer me that one if you will.

Another question I have, somewhat related to the first, is how come we don't feel that our kids are safe any more. Once again, I go back to my own childhood, growing up on the streets of the Bronx. We walked to school and nobody ever worried about being attacked on the way. In school, there weren't any kids with guns trying to shoot classmates and teachers. After school, we played on the street with no adult supervision and nobody thought twice about. So, where did all these crazy kids with guns come from? Where did all the pedophiles come from?

Another thing that puzzles me off and on is the energy problem. I say "off and on" because the energy problem seems to come and go. Everyone agrees that we should do something about becoming energy independent. When gas hit $4 a gallon last summer this was one of our most urgent problems and a big issue in the presidential campaign. As of now, with gas a little below $3 a gallon, the urgency seems to have disappeared. We're concerned about health care and greenhouse gases, but energy has taken a back seat.

We've been talking about energy independence since at least back to the 1970's and nobody, whether Democrats or Republicans, has done anything about it. Seems to me that in all that time it would have been possible to put the "experts" to work and come up with at least some ideas. As it is, something will happen, maybe with Iran, gas prices will shoot up again, and we'll be back at square one. Explain that to me.

Then, backtracking to the State budget, I ask: what has happened to the once great state of California? When I emigrated here from New York in the 1950's, I did so because the climate was good (no more shoveling snow), the people were laid-back and friendly, everything was moving forward, the education system was the nation's best and was affordable, California was a great place to live. Now look where we are, in a shambles. There are newspaper and magazine articles about how bad California has become, about our "buffoonish" Governor and our "dysfunctional" legislature. And these articles are all too true. What has happened? Can we get back to being at least a pretty good place to live. I sincerely hope so.

Observations has some more questions, such as: why can't they make good movies any more? What happened to all that stimulus money? Where did all those "toxic assets" go? How come they're always doing road work around Sun City? Oh, yes, there's still that perennial question: where did all those people parked outside the Lodge go? E-mail any answers to mgreensuncity@yahoo.com

October 2009 Observations

After writing an "Observations" saying there's no place like home, I see that a couple of months later we were off on another trip: New York, Ireland, London. It was a good trip, but I was once again glad to be home.

Observations Goes on Another Trip

Yes, Beverly and I were on the road again, this time to visit our son and his family in Ireland, preceded by a stay in New York (with my sister Phyllis) and followed by a last visit to London. Here, before I forget, are some of the trip highlights. When I exited LaGuardia Airport out onto the street I was hit in the face by something I'd nearly forgotten---that dread East Coast humidity. So that's why, I thought, I'd left New York for California (one of the reasons anyway).

Despite the humidity, New York has its compensations. I don't know of any eating place quite like a New York, more specifically Long Island, diner. In past years, my sister Phyllis had taken us to the legendary Seaford Diner, but it had changed ownership so this year it was the East Bay Diner. The purpose of a diner is to give you a lot of food at a reasonable price with a minimum of fuss. As soon as we were seated, a busboy put glasses of water and an appetizer on our table. Within a minute Virginia, a typical no-nonsense diner waitress, came to take our order. The dinner (cost under $15) included soup, salad, entrée and dessert.

The soup arrived almost at once, and then the rest of the meal. Beverly chose lamb chops and I chose pork chops for our entrees. My plate held four pork chops, large ones. After soup and salad I was able to eat one. But I didn't skip dessert, a large slice of chocolate cake. I forget what my sister's entrée was, but she had a large Danish for dessert and ate half of it. When we left we were laden down with boxes of food.

The daily forecast for Irish weather is "variable," but this doesn't begin to describe it. When Beverly and I went into Galway (where our son Chris lives) for the afternoon, we had rain, sun, clouds, wind and calm, all within the space of a few minutes. I was kept busy opening and closing my jacket, putting my hood up and down and flipping my sun glasses. Regardless of the weather, it's always nice to come into the Busker (not "Buster") Brown restaurant and order the savory Guinness stew---beef and mashed potatoes in a delicious gravy topped by a flaky biscuit. We ate in many restaurants during our trip but Busker's stands out.

I mentioned that we made a last visit to London. We'd previously been there 16 years ago, in 1993. There were some changes. London has become very expensive. It doesn't help that our dollar is less than the pound, which was worth over $1.60 when we were there. In Ireland, the Euro was worth a little over $1.40. I decided the best thing to do was to follow my son Chris's example and to think of the pound (and the Euro) as just dollars. So a $20 meal was $20, not over $32.

London has also become a very diverse city with people of all kinds and, correspondingly, eating places of all kinds. In fact, it's not easy to find "typical" English food any more. We did discover a restaurant with roast beef and Yorkshire pudding and a pub with steak and ale pie. We also found a kind of fast food pub chain, Shakespeare's Head and also Weatherspoon's (maybe connected), with very reasonable prices (see above) and not bad food.

Most importantly, the old London sights are all still there: the Tower, Westminster Abbey, St. Paul's, the British Museum and the art galleries. We could get one of those red double-decker buses (they're also still there) from our hotel to Trafalgar Square so after sitting in the sun (our London weather was good) for a while we went to the National Gallery. We'd been there before, but I'd forgotten how many great paintings it had. There were the Gainsboroughs and Turners and lots of English nobles and generals but also Impressionists, Michelangelo and Rembrandt. There were also Van Gogh's sunflowers, cypress trees and straw chair. (We'd been at the Van Gogh Museum in Amsterdam in May and I'd wondered where they were).

After a couple of hours of art looking we were tired and followed the signs to the gallery café. Art gallery cafes are not always that good, tending to be crowded and noisy, but the National Gallery Café was not crowded, quiet, spacious and airy (most welcome after the somewhat stuffy art rooms). And we were able to get another traditional dish, fish and chips, very good.

But the highlight of our London visit undoubtedly was Beverly's reunion with two English friends, Sheila Leake and Janet Hart, after I don't know how many years. We spent the day with them, having lunch in Greenwich at Weatherspoon's. Then we rode the Eye, the 450-foot high Ferris wheel, which goes around in half and hour and provides spectacular views of London. We had good, if variable, weather on our ride, mostly sunny, a rain shower and a rainbow.

Good grief, I almost forgot THE highlight of our trip, seeing Chris and his wife Flindie and our two-year old grandson Logan and one-year old granddaughter Stephanie. As readers know, Observations is, like Fox, fair and balanced so when I say these are the cutest grandchildren in Ireland you know this is true. Okay, I'll end with that.

November 2009 Observations---on Things I Really Hate

Thanksgiving is fast approaching and on its heels comes Christmas, the season when everyone is supposed to be jolly and of good cheer. So I thought I'd seize the day and while there's time have an Observations on "Things I Really Hate." These are not merely "Life's Little Annoyances" (LLA's) but LLA's doubled or maybe tripled.

Readers know that I've taken a few trips this year so let's get this out of the way first: I hate anything having to do with airports and airplanes. No need to go into detail here (I've already done so in previous columns); an overview will suffice. Trip delays, extra baggage charges, airplane food, no food at all, no leg room at all, the security (ha, ha) line, taking off your shoes, etc., etc.

Next, a couple of things connected with but not confined to airplane flights. Firstly, the international plot to prevent people from getting into things by encasing all objects in an impenetrable plastic that cannot be breached by any means short of a jackhammer or dynamite. This includes anything given to you on an airplane, also food items, medications, razors, batteries, CDs and every type of toy. Secondly, a lesser evil but still bad enough, those tiny earphones given to you on airplanes and that also come with CD players and little radios, guaranteed to fall out of your ears in less than 30 seconds.

I see I'm still suffering from air flight trauma so let's shift to things I hate in day-to-day life I hate all phone calls from strangers trying to sell something or soliciting a donation, no matter how worthy the cause, especially when they come at dinnertime or when I'm expecting an important call from someone else that I do know. My special hate is reserved for those ask, "Is Martin there?" or who addresses me as "Martin." I'm always tempted to say, "When do you want me to come over for dinner? You seem to know me well enough to call me by my first name so I'm sure you'll want to invite me."

I hate sneezing at inopportune times, and when is there an opportune time for sneezing? I especially hate it when I sneeze while driving and so have to reflexively close my eyes when I'm trying to keep them open and on the road. I hate politicians on general principle and California politicians, who've gotten our state in such a mess, in particular. I hate all entertainers of no discernible talent who are paid outrageous amounts of money for doing nothing of value to anyone. That includes most of them. The same holds true for most athletes, although athletes do have to perform. Still, the money they're paid to perform had gone beyond all reasonable bounds.

It goes without saying that I hate television commercials. I especially hate any commercial in which babies or young children instruct stupid adults in how to invest their money or what nutritional foods to eat or anything else. On a somewhat related note, I hate any commercial or TV show in which the husband and/or father is portrayed as a stupid jerk. I hate commercials showing scruffy-looking guys dribbling ketchup and food particles all over while eating huge greasy-looking hamburgers. I wouldn't go into places serving these hamburgers for fear that I'd slip on the greasy, food-stained floor as soon as I entered.

Finally, I'm reminded of something else I really hate because it just happened; my computer, which was fine half an hour ago, refused to go online, meaning I had to turn it off and then on again and then get back on (it did). Maybe just a LLA, but I still hate it, especially as it happens several times a week.

Okay, I think I've vented enough for now. Next month, in keeping with the season, a kindler, gentler Observations.

December 2009 Observations---on Christmas

My birthday is on December 30th so when I was a kid I'd be given a present (one only) and be told, "Merry Christmas and happy birthday." It's a wonder that this didn't warp my personality and that I became the nice, pleasant well-balanced guy that everyone in Sun City thinks I am. (They do, don't they?).

At Christmas-time someone is bound to ask the question: what are the names of Santa's reindeers? Write this down and memorize it. The reindeers, there are eight, are: Dasher and Dancer, Prancer and Vixen, Comet and Cupid, Donder and Blitzen. Then of course there's the late-comer, Rudolph with his red nose. Along with this, the gifts from the song, "The Twelve Days of Christmas," are: a partridge in a pear tree, two turtle doves, three French hens, four calling birds, five golden rings, six geese a-laying, seven swans a-swimming, eight maids a-milking, nine ladies dancing, ten lords a-leaping, eleven pipers piping and twelve drummers drumming. And, in case anyone asks: Snow White's seven dwarfs are: Doc, Grumpy, Sneezy, Happy, Bashful, Sleepy and Dopey.

I grew up in the Bronx in the 1930's, the time of the real Depression, so we (my sister and myself) didn't get a whole lot of presents. The "big" presents I received came from my great-uncle, who lived in a far-off place across the Hudson called New Jersey and who, like Santa, came only once a year, at Christmas. I remember that my three "big" presents for three years in a row were a microscope, a science set and, the biggest, an Erector set. My lab and workshop was our kitchen table. My great-uncle was a barber and bought comic books to keep in his shop for his kid customers. He'd also bring a bunch of these at Christmas and they'd probably be worth a fortune today. Needless to say, my mother threw them all out, thus ruining my chance to become a multi-millionaire.

Santa's reindeer come from the poem "A Visit from Saint Nicholas," otherwise known as "T'was the Night Before Christmas." The poem was originally published anonymously in 1823 and then, should you be asked, by Clement Clarke Moore in 1844.

The poem not only gave us the reindeer but a lot of other things about Christmas, such as Santa's physical appearance (plump and jolly), the night of his visit, the mode of his transportation, and his bringing of toys for children.

Is there a Santa Claus? Well, Virginia and others, I'd say it's a matter of belief. When our youngest son was six or seven he'd begun to doubt, but then he told us he'd heard Santa up on our roof and so he knew there was a Santa (at least for another year).

A Bavarian illustrator named Thomas Nast drew over 2,000 cartoon of Santa Claus based on Moore's poem for Harper's Weekly magazine. Nast also gave Santa a home at the North Pole, a workshop with elves and a list of good and bad kids.

Christmas is mainly for kids and when ours were small they'd come into our bedroom in the middle of the night and ask if it was time to get up yet. So Christmas day was spent in a semi-fog, especially if I'd spent the night before putting together one or more toys, trying to decipher directions given in Sanskrit

If you've been able to name the eight reindeer, the twelve gifts for the twelve days of Christmas and the guy who wrote "A Visit from Saint Nicholas," someone might ask you, "So how come Santa Claus wears that red suit?" In 1931, a Swedish commercial artist named Haddon Sundblom was commissioned by the Coca-Cola company to draw a Coke-drinking

Santa Claus. Coca-Cola wanted Santa to be in a bright red Coca-Cola colored outfit and that completed his current image.

I just remembered that it's not politically correct to even say "Christmas" any more. You're supposed to say "Season's Greetings" or "Happy Holidays" or "Happy Winter Celebration" or something generic like that. I'll take the risk and wish everyone a "Merry Christmas" plus a "Happy Hanakuh," a "Happy Kwanza" and, for Seinfeld fans, a "Happy Festivus." And be sure to remember the names of those reindeer.

Observations on My Father

I'm not sure when I wrote it, but I wanted to end this book with an "Observations" I wrote about my father. I guess you could say that my father is my hero. In a way, he was just an ordinary guy. He never became rich or famous. He never went to college. He served in the Navy after World War I, then he became a plumber. He married my mother and they stayed together for over 60 years. They had two children, my sister Phyllis and myself. He made it through the Great Depression, taking whatever jobs he could get, including one with the WPA, then worked out of town through World War II, then after the war was finally able to come back to New York, where he worked until his sixties, then took another job, in the supply room of a lamp company, until he finally retired in his seventies. No matter what, he provided for his family. In our current world of permissiveness, self-indulgence," selfishness, greed and egotism, I often think of my father. He was a hero.

My father Joseph Green was born in New York City just before the turn of the century. His father came to this country from Poland because tailors were needed to stitch uniforms for our soldiers in the Spanish-American War.

The story in our family about how we got our name is this. When the immigration person at Ellis Island saw my grandfather's long, unpronounceable Polish name, he asked the relative, or family friend, accompanying him what his name was. The name was Greenberg or Greenblatt or Greensomething-or-other. The immigration man was for simplicity, so he shortened it to Green and that's how our family dynasty started.

From all reports, my grandfather, although he must have done okay in America because he became a landlord, wasn't a generous man. My father was the oldest of seven children. His education ended before he finished high school so that he could go to work and help support the family.

I don't know what jobs my father had in his teens and 20's but I do know that sometime after WWI he had a stint in the Navy. He had a good job in the paymaster's office and could have made the Navy his career but after a few years returned to being a civilian. Maybe he got tired of being out at sea. Maybe he had a premonition that he'd meet my mother. They were married 73 years ago, in 1927.

By this time, my father must have entered the occupation he'd work at until he retired (the first time); he was a plumber. I was born in 1929, just after the stock market crash, and my sister in 1935. I'm sure that during the depression years of the 1930's my father's life was a struggle to put bread on his family's table. I'm not sure how he managed, but he did. I know he took any job he could find. When the WPA was established, he worked for that. To pay, or help pay, the rent, he fixed the plumbing in the buildings owned by our landlord, Mondschein, whose name I still remember because then he was such an important figure in our lives.

Somehow during these years, my mother, my sister and myself always "went to the mountains" during the summers to get away from the city heat. This meant staying in a ramshackle boarding house where the women gathered in the kitchen to do the cooking, but it was away from the heat. We usually went away with my cousins. On weekends, my father and uncle would come up by bus from the city. We were glad to see my uncle, but when my father came, always with some candy or toy, all the kids would rush up and climb all over him.

Our family's economic standing, like many others, didn't take a turn for the better until the advent of WWII. Even before the start of the war, my father started going out of town to work on war-related projects. The first time was in 1939 when he left the Bronx and went south to Florida. (For years, we had a little seashell lamp from there as a memento). From there, he went to such places as Oklahoma, Michigan and Oak Ridge, Tennessee, where he worked on something having to do with the atomic bomb.

Wherever my father worked, his bosses liked him. He was always the first on his job to be hired and the last to be let go (the jobs always ended, then it was on to the next one). The landladies at the boarding houses where he stayed all loved him and saved their best delicacies for him.

Even after WWII ended, my father had to go out of town to find work. I remember that he worked a long time in Pittsburgh, from where he could occasionally come to the Bronx to see us. Finally, it must have been in the 1950's, New York City had a building boom and he was able to come home to stay.

As I look back on it, my father spent the years from when he was 40 to when he was in his mid-50's away from his family and on the road. This must have been a tremendous hardship, but I never heard him complain about it.

My father retired from plumbing when he was 69. Then he went to work for a lamp factory way out in Queens. This meant he had to travel about an hour and a half one way on two subways. He was in charge of the factory's supply room. He began to collect spare parts not otherwise used and put these together to make elaborate lamps. Soon everyone in our family, and most of our friends, had beautiful lamps in their homes.

When he was 79, the long subway rides finally became too much and my father retired again, this time for good. Until a few years ago, he and my mother alternated between their apartment in the Bronx for most of the year and a residential hotel in Miami over the winter. During all this time, my father resisted moving into a senior place because he didn't want to be with "all those old people." When he was 96, he finally gave in.

Until about 10 years ago, my father and mother would pay us yearly visits in California and my kids felt the same way about my father as we kids did when he'd visit us in the mountains some 50 years ago. I think my father is a great man. I'm sure he'll live to be 100 and I hope many years after that. He deserves to. As mentioned above, I never heard him talk about self-fulfillment. He's done it.